Hot Pink **YOU**NIVERSITY

Ignite ...
Your Life

Ann Murgatroyd-Soe
&
Christie Gause-Bemis

Ignite Your Life
Live Life with Passion, Purpose and Play

Ann Murgatroyd-Soe and Christie Gause-Bemis

Copyright 2016 Hot Pink YOUniversity
www.hotpinkyou.com

ISBN: 978-1-944878-24-5

We dedicate this book to all of those women
who supported us, encouraged us, laughed with us, and
believed in us. You have taught us more than you know.

And to our families, loving and with us all the way.

Thank you!

INTRODUCTION

This is not your average self-growth book. If you picked us up because you were hoping to "find yourself," we are here to tell you, "*You* already have." March over to the nearest mirror, make sure the light is on, and take a gigantic look. There *You* are. No, we are not into the *finding* game, we are into the *fire-up-your-life* game. That's right, big gorgeous, illuminating fires. Your life, amped up, living boldly and loving what you wake up to every single day.

In a nation that spends close to $1 billion in the area of self-help and self-growth books, we know there are people out there, women people, needing someone to market a book to them that has "all the answers." A book that if you pick it up and just hold it, promises to make you feel better. A book just waiting to go home with you and be your new best friend.

And we are here to say "bullshit!"

You know why we say "bullshit"? Because for years, we **were** those women. And truth be told, sometimes we still are. There are many days when we walk into that bookstore, gradually swanker over to the self-help section when we're feeling sad and lowdown. We run our fingers along the beautiful spines and pick up those books brimming with hope and expectancy. And, we choose the book that offers the message we know, we just know, will make it all right. If you want proof of those purchases, just stop on over to one of our homes to see the mini libraries we've established.

So with that said, this book is not going to coddle you and handle you with kid gloves. If you are into that thing, I suggest putting us down right now. We will see you back in a year or so.

What this book won't do.

This book is not going to hang out in the past and heal your traumas and pay homage to those people who have done you wrong like some sappy country song.

This book is not going to place blame on others about where you are or how you feel. The woman in the mirror will take full responsibility and acceptance of self, of choices and of her past.

This book is not into fixing other people. We suggest, in fact, when you get into that head space of seeking solutions for others so they may change or be a "better" person, that you mind your own business—which leads us to:

What this Playbook will do

If you are into:

- Living on Fire!
- Claiming your desires
- Using your mess as your messenger
- Creating possibilities
- Having limitless beliefs
- Being good in your skin
- Living in the here and the now
- Being strong, being determined, being YOU
- Creating more passion, more purpose and much more play!
  And…
- Connecting with other people who want to do the same

Then you are in the right place.

The women of Hot Pink YOUniversity say it is time for you to:

- Take 100% full responsibility for you and the path you are on

Introduction

- Focus on you first and *then* others
- Create a promise to yourself for self-love and self-worth
- Live the life you dream every damn day
- Wake to your life each morning with a big "Ahhhhh!"

Are YOU into that kind of thing?
Let's Ignite YOUR Life!

Becoming a Hot Pink Woman

A Hot Pink Woman lives life out loud! She is ready and willing to find and embrace her depth, complexity, passion, and power. She honors and values herself equal to others in her life. She is creating a life that will fulfill her wishes, dreams, needs, and wants.

A Hot Pink Woman is a Firestarter!

She has the combustible juice to ignite a life of passion, pleasure, prosperity, and vibrant health.

She is a succulent, sensational, sensual woman who is doing and being everything she desires and will spark others to do the same.

Dear Succulent Woman on the Path to Becoming a Firestarter,

We are so happy to be on this journey with you, lovingly holding you in energy and ready to guide the way to living a Hot Pink Life and becoming, what we call, a true Firestarter. It won't always be easy, but it is so worth it at this time in your life when you are ready and open to wanting more. It is time to bust open into a life you are meant to live.

Now you know what it means to become Hot Pink Woman. This is a mindset shift, a way of living your life unapologetically. This Playbook will spark your curiosity and put you on the same path that other women take in our Woman on Fire Program.

Women dive in deep on these issues when they work with us. Throughout this Playbook, we will share our stories and stories of our Hot Pink tribe as well. Women *are* their stories. We learn from our mothers, aunties, friends, and sisters through our stories. It is a powerful way to make us feel connected, normal, and whole. As we share our Hot Pink stories, be mindful of the experiences that are similar and tug at the core of your own story. We encourage you to write your story, and share it with the other women in your life. Become aware of the differences and many variations that women offer to the world. We are all a rich tapestry of colored experiences. There is an importance of opening those stories up, revealing ourselves and being raw and vulnerable with other women in our lives.

Enjoy the journey…it will be HOT!

With Joy and Overflowing Abundance,
Ann Murgatroyd-Soe & Christie Gause-Bemis

Sister seekers, women of wonder, beautiful adventurers—Join us on this journey as you tune into and resonate with the voices of Hot Pink YOUniversity. Add your own cadence of self-discovery. Throw yourself into the center of your YOUniverse, fan the flame of your future, and illuminate your radiance. C'mon Woman, Light *Your* Fire!

Introduction

The Women of Hot Pink YOUniversity!

In most books, the author bio is a short blurb found at the back of the book with just the basics. At Hot Pink YOUniversity (HPYOU), we believe in the undeniable power of sharing stories. We all learn best from story. We want you to know who we are and what shaped us. So, on that note, we will start by introducing ourselves!

Ann Murgatroyd-Soe, MSSW, LCSW

"I am an adventurer, traveler, writer, lover, mother, sister, friend on an amazing journey in life that has lead me to the realization that brilliant things happen when likeminded people gather together. This is at the core of the HPYOU experience. Life is bursting with juicy, wild, succulent moments that when honored will shape and forever change us. I am living out loud and am passionate about encouraging others to do the same."

The Story of Ann

I am Ann, Annie, Annabelle, BellsABob (thanks for that creativity, Mom!) Annie Banannie, and Murgy, short for my maiden name of Murgatroyd. Yes, as in "Heavens to Murgatroyd." (actually, Murgy 2…because Dad was our number one).

I am a woman that "lives life out loud!" It has become one of my favorite phrases. I have always had it in me, but didn't really know how to genuinely do it until midlife. I love being a woman and all that it encompasses. I come from a long line of strong women who knew and lived in their power. Who were "good in their own skin." Women who taught—and showed me—that women can do and be anything they desire and succeed at it. I listened, learned, and wanted to have that too. Oh, I had bits of it here and there, but like most of us, I had a lot to learn and a lot in my way!

I am a writer. Since I can remember, I have written my way through the most powerful times in life…the inspirational and the devastating alike. I love the sound and the energy of words. I am a lyrical lover of sorts. I am a poet. I use my words to inspire women when I talk, teach, sing, play and share.

> *"I'm a succulent woman, a strong woman, a say it like it is kinda woman. I'm a sassy woman, a serious woman, a proud to be a sister kinda woman. I'm a real woman, a round woman, a diggin' my curves kinda woman. I'm a driven woman, a dancin' woman, a goin' downtown kinda woman. I'm a wild woman, a wise woman, my Mama's daughter kinda woman. I'm an adventurous woman, a daring woman, a travelin' around the world kinda woman. I'm a soulful woman, a sensuous woman, a takin' care of business kinda woman. I am!"*

I *love* that a woman is all this and more. I believe with all I am that we are not to be ashamed or apologetic for our depth, our vision, our complexity, our passion, our power. I live, speak, and behave this belief! It is how I live out loud. It is what I have come to know and want to show. I am one of the bodacious broads of Hot Pink YOUniversity.

So who and what contributed to who I am today?

I am a first born. I am the daughter of Dave and Gloria, the big sister of Crystal and Mary, the mother of Grant, and the lover of Joel. I grew up in a middle class family with a solid set of values including family first, work for what you want, help those you love, those you know, and even those you don't know, and make a difference in the world. Being the quintessential

Introduction

first born, I took these very seriously. I lived under the, "be a good girl/do the right responsible thing" motto and let me say, I did it well!

My early childhood was pretty all American and apple pie like. I can tell you when that changed. I was six years old and my maternal grandma died unexpectedly in her sleep of an aneurism in her early fifties. My world changed in so many ways from that day. It was my first experience with death. It was also in some ways the death of my mom as well. She was different after that so everything was different after that. So much of it I didn't understand for several years. I just knew things weren't right or ok and it shaped me.

On a sunny summer day when I was nine years old I got clarity in a can and remember every vivid moment of it. I had been off on some outdoor adventure as I so often was, on the beautiful two hundred acres of woodlands that I had the great fortune to grow up on. I was likely imagining that I was a Native American girl who was a warrior along with the men in her tribe…this was one of my favorite images! I came rushing in to the house and grabbed a Coke can from the kitchen counter to take a big swig. I was hit with the power of not cola but booze. It knocked me back and then it really hit me. *This* was my Mom's soda, filled with alcohol. She was an alcoholic, this is what had happened to her, and this is what had made it all different!

Now my "be a good girl/do the right responsible thing" belief really kicked into hyperdrive! I became a mini mom of sorts to my sisters, and in many ways, the caretaker of our home and family. Thus started the journey of my womanhood marked by the driving force of making sure everyone and everything was ok. I grew up so focused on my "world" that in many ways I got lost in the mix. My definition of self was in how well those I loved were doing rather than who I really was in my own skin.

While I had many amazing times in my young adult life, this dynamic set the stage for many experiences of loss, disappointment, and very unbalanced relationships…especially with men! I fell easily and deeply in love with men that needed to be rescued, parented, even saved at times…or so I thought! I rarely found my own desires, wishes, needs, or passions being met in my intimate relationships, and somehow I just accepted that as how it was to be. I will tell you though that deep down inside I was kicking and clawing my way to the life I really wanted to have. I knew I was a free spirit, wild child adventurer by nature, and that the paths I chose were more about that fear based, do-the-right-thing dynamic, than about who I really was.

Be assured, I found many amazing and fulfilling times in my life as I "grew myself up" to be a college-educated, professional woman, therapist, wife, mother, colleague, adult friend, and community activist. For all intents and purposes I had succeeded at creating exactly the life the "good girl/do the right responsible thing" would want for herself. All the bells and whistles of a wonderful life—only there was a growing sense that those bells and whistles were not creating much in the way of music for me!

I am a lover of music. I gotta sing and dance.

And I was feeling like a wallflower at the dance of my own life. I know now that I would l have stayed in this safe, solid, sensible situation if it weren't the start of a series of tragedies to fall on myself and my family.

On April 22, 1999, my world was once again rocked in a way that I knew everything was and would forever be different and that nothing was ok. The phone rang in my office during a client session…unheard of so I was caught a bit off guard. When I answered and was told it was a police officer, I stopped breathing. I will never forget the words that came next. "Mrs. Soe, your parents have been in a serious car accident, and we

Introduction

need you to come to the ER right away. Do you have someone who can drive you?"

The world was spinning, and I couldn't catch my breath or feel the ground under my feet. My father who was the most brilliant and loving man I had ever met and truly a best friend to me died that day when a car shot out across four lanes of highway traffic and directly into his truck. My mother was gravely injured, with multiple severe traumas but alive. It is a known fact that my father shielded her from the violent blow in his last moments alive. This would be a final symbol of how deeply he loved her and how he cared for her throughout their marriage. She had a tragic and vulnerable side to her, and he always kept her as safe and secure as he could.

Let me share, that my mother who was on her own journey, went from being in my eyes, a vulnerable, dependent, and fearful woman to one of the strongest women I have ever known following the accident and through her recovery. She showed a courage and inner strength I would likely never have known had she not lost my Dad and faced all that was yet to come in her life.

So, just as my innocence had gone that summer day with the Coke can, my illusion of the life I had built for myself and my family was gone with that call. What followed was life changing in its tragedy and in the new level of clarity that began to unfold for me. I knew I was on a trajectory that was going to once again shape me. Only this time, I felt a slow rumbling, a growing voice inside that showed me that it took something so unthinkably devastating to move me…really move me to get out of my own way. I began to truly feel my own emotions first. I realized I was not ok and that I needed to reach out to others now for the kind of love and help I had always given. I was not going to make it through if I didn't change me. As e. e. cummings says, "It takes courage to grow up and turn out to be who you really are."

I made lots of good changes and began experimenting with who I really was, what I really liked, what I really wanted, and how I was going to learn to live in ways that gave me that. Yet, even then, I often fell back into old patterns. Looking back, I realize that the delicate dance that unfolded after 1999—just when I settled into my life again—the life that was safe and solid but not succulent or sensational…the next tragedies would strike. At the time, I didn't really see the connection and wondered why these terrible losses kept happening. Now, I see that each of those losses—of my Mother to ALS six years to the exact day that my dad died and then two years later my beautiful, sparkling angel of a nephew died in his sleep at three years old—were ripping me open to the real, raw, ravaging nature of the cycle of life.

I lost so much of what I knew and had to decide if I would paint a new canvas in my life or put away the colors and dry up. It was no longer a rumbling, but a roar, and I knew I had to start living my life as I truly desired. I was going to find out who I really was and this was the start of living life out loud for me! I could no longer define myself only by my relationships. Life had shown me that security was an illusion, and that I was meant to be that visionary, the adventurer from my childhood imaginings in that beautiful 200 acres of woodlands.

You see, it was with the clarity in a can and a life-stopping call—which brought all the pain, suffering, learning, yearning, reaching, and growing—that I was birthed into this world as the woman I am truly meant to be.

In the words of Joseph Campbell, "We must be willing to give up the life we planned in order to live the life that is waiting for us."

I have done this! I am living my life out loud. I am Ann…a succulent, sensational, sensual, wild woman who is doing and being everything that I desire! It really is a magnificent place to be!

Introduction

Christie Gause-Bemis, MSW, LCSW

There has got to be something more…more joy, more love, more peace, more juice, more gratitude, more jazz and pizzazz! I am a believer in more. It is with gratitude of what I already have in life that I stand on and shout for "more". More for me and more for all of you, the sisters who join me on your own journey for more. I am a momma, an artist, a sister, and a gatherer of women. HPYOU allows me to live my life's purpose, to carry out my deepest passions and to discover the connection of play. To live my life ignited!

The Story of Christie

On a Clear Day You Can See Yourself: Turning the Life You Have Into the Life You Want by Sonya Freidman was the first self-help book I purchased. It was during my junior year in college, midterm week with papers due—and I had a due date for myself at the time. It was about time I got my shit together and did some serious excavation of the soul and be the woman I was meant to be.

I had just been most decidedly dumped by a man I loved intensely. The fact that it had taken him a full year and a half to come to the conclusion that I had at the start of our relationship, "He is too good for me," was pretty incredible. I sank at the end of the breakup, raw, in pain, and hopeless. I could say it started with that boy, but it was much sooner than that. He was just the catalyst to unearth the rest of the story.

I grew up outside of town, "in the country" with sun-kissed skin, long days playing outside in the woods and the fields of my childhood. It was a good childhood. My older sister, Michelle, was ever the leader and the "good" girl in our family. I was sandwiched between her and my younger brother whom everyone adored. I was supposed to be a boy, the second after Michelle, so I came to realize that to get my dad's attention, praise, and love, I needed to hunt squirrels with a pellet gun, take my own fish off the line, ride motorbikes, and embrace the masculine. It worked, for awhile. I do believe my dad loved me in his perfectly, imperfect way. And, my mother often stated I was "beautiful," "amazing" and she loved me, there is something about a girl needing that love and praise from her daddy. And it didn't help that I was born with a sensitive, shy, and "please, please notice me" temperament. This did not fit well with the kind of love my dad had the potential of dosing out.

In second grade, my parents divorced and my childhood, as I knew it, came to an abrupt halt. Security and simpler times flew out the window. I discovered that I was the only person in the greater Plover, Wisconsin area, with divorced parents when a student asked me, "Is it true your parents got a divorce?" while I was standing at the front of class during introductions on my first day. Insert class-wide audible gasp. I found my way back to my seat through teared up eyes, as my teacher said that I did not have to answer. There was shame in divorce in my small, predominately Polish Catholic town. I felt that shame deeply, and it confirmed my own thoughts of myself: one, I do not fit in with others, and two, I don't deserve to fit in. I also knew this, very distinctly at my young age- things happen for a reason. I sensed there was a deep knowing I needed in my life brought to me through these struggles. I did not know how I would use this knowledge, I just knew I *would* someday.

When I think back, it leaves me with both an icky feeling and a sense of amazement. I hardly recognize that skinny, tan, shy girl of my past. Today, I am outspoken, confident, secure in who I am—regardless of what is happening around me.

Introduction

Like most people, my transformation came out of a gift of—as I like to call it, a shit sandwich. My beautiful, confident, oh-so-much-wiser, good girl, brown-eyed sister Michelle was diagnosed with a brain tumor the year I graduated from college. Prior to surgery, the doctor thought it was benign. We thought this would be a minor blip on the screen of life. Get through this, and we could move on to growing old together, raising our children, and sitting long, lazy summer evenings at the campfire. Three days after her operation the tumor was found to be malignant. Gone were the future dreams sisters create. Our lives shifted from thriving to surviving with a word…cancer. The next year was filled with radiation and chemo, as my sister slowly lost various functions. First a limp, then her arm hung in a funny way. The ability to self-care vanished as did her will to survive. Michelle died three months after my son, Lucas, was born, and my world shattered down. I left the funeral, saying goodbye for one last time as they closed the casket, and I sat at a street corner in my car, incredulous that the world continued to go on as if nothing just happened here. Yet, the world did move on—and, eventually I moved forward as well. I had to, what other choices were there?

During the year after her death, I felt intensely. Isolation. Anger. Disconnect from spirit. I did not know what to do with this intensity. It was unbearable and it broke me open. Through therapy, retreats and journaling, I emerged. I jumped back onto the path that I had left when I became scared in college. A year after my sister's death, I left a marriage that did not work for either one of us. And, thinking death was hard, it did little to prepare me for what divorce felt like. I remember reading in a book during that time that in order to get back to myself, I needed to be prepared to lose everything. And, I was.

This began years of getting back into my artwork, something I had left behind along the way. Reading for pleasure. Connecting with the women in my life and cultivating deep friendships. I started a book club. I went on silent retreats, drumming retreats, spiritual retreats. Out of the deep despair, I emerged reborn, and stronger. I was the story of the lotus, bound in the muck, it moves towards the surface, seeking out the sun. When it breaks through the surface of the water, it opens, pure, white, untainted from the mud.

Life had handed me what I call, shit sandwiches. It was not wrapped in a pretty bow and tissue paper. It was a big ol' pile of shit! And, it was up to me to turn that gift into something for myself. I cultivated that time that I had as a single woman into the rich loamy soil of my current life. Every day, I choose better over bitter. I shaped my life to what it is today, something I have great pride in…Me.

I believe we all can grow larger and more radiant from the shit gifts that life inevitably has in store for each of us. I believe we can have great support from the women around us. I believe we are wondrous beings with limitless potential.

There you have it—The Women of Hot Pink YOUniversity!!

In co-creating Hot Pink YOUniversity, we are very mindful of what we have been through as women, of what we have overcome. <u>Our</u> stories are <u>your</u> stories. We all have "shit sandwiches" in life. Many of us choose to go through those and come out in ways that grow us. Some of us still need encouragement that the best is yet to come. There is always a lesson in every breath of life we take. Here's to remembering that the greatest untapped resource on this planet is ourselves.

The Story of Hot Pink YOUniversity

In 2005, we had a vision to gather women on a transformational retreat to Costa Rica. Christie had been gathering women through her book club and in evening Soup and Soulfood gatherings, two hour workshops with a warm bowl of soup and using multi-media, art, videos, music, dance and conversation. Ann had been gathering women through her private practice as a psychotherapist and teacher for support, mental

Introduction

health, personal growth and wellness. On a scouting trip to Costa Rica, Life's Journey Retreats, LLC was born. It was a company name we created to sign on the line on a contract with a travel company. It was zen. It was flowery. Life's Journey Retreats exemplified what we desired for women who would seek to work with us on their transformations.

As we shared in our stories, life had handed us some shit sandwiches along the way. We were busy women leading busy lives. Zen and peace were what we were craving at that time. As our babies grew into fully functioning, independent humans, our evolution as women began to unfold. Some amazing, brilliant, bold, tragic, gut-wrenching experiences happened for us after the creation of Life's Journey Retreats.

How Life's Journey Retreats evolved into Hot Pink YOUniversity…

Hot Pink YOUniversity began when we gathered with a small group of women on a cold January day in Wisconsin. We were creating some heat as we answered the invite to a sex toy party perusing lubes and massage oils, toys and lingerie, to enhance sexuality and sensuality. If you have ever been through Wisconsin in January, watched the weather channel about Wisconsin in January, or just understand the climate of the north woods, heat and Wisconsin winter are an pairing. That January day, we were sparked as, we created a cauldron of ideas, laughter, and desires **to be and have more!** We discussed our lives, our journeys, and as the event came to a close, we realized that we had some *"stuff"* to share. Hot Pink YOUniversity alchemized from that gathering to create heat and fire in our lives and to spark that in the lives of all women seeking to understand, grow, be, and have a passionately plugged in life!

The women of Hot Pink YOUniversity have many roles, mammas and aunties, sisters and friends, daughters and lovers.

We have a variety of relationship experiences: married, divorced, and remarried with blended families. We are psychotherapists, mentors, adventurers, and all around bodacious broads. Both of us has been through our own unique stories with many lessons learned. We have thrown ourselves into the center of our YOUniverse, our fire, and we are living large.

We passionately believe *You* can have a life of abundance and juiciness. Yes, *You!* Okay, let's wash, rinse, and repeat…

You Can Exist in a Passionate Life of Abundance!

The society we live in tends to create boxes and limitations and judgments. As women of Hot Pink YOUniversity, we insists on living large, outside the box, with limitless possibilities and to the beat of your own drum. A drum that beats to the rhythm of your desires!

Imagine this: Your life is being stripped away of all limits, judgments, and boxes. Now imagine that you adorn yourself with limitless dreams and ideas, gratitude and joy, beauty and pleasure. Imagine that you walk into any room and have people recognize what a confident, sexy, juicy, and succulent woman you are. When others see your inner light radiating and exploding from you, they want exactly what you are having. You. Yes, yes, yes, *You* are the best and brightest that you can possibly be. You are way too big for your britches, loving life, and full of succulent possibilities. Now, that is a *Hot, Hot, Hot*, Pink Woman!

Hot Pink YOUniversity Passion Statement

A smokin' hot life. We all want it! A woman who throws herself into her own fire and the center of her YOUniverse is a woman who will radiate heat, love, and joy with everyone and everything she touches. A turned on woman turns on the YOUniverse!

Introduction

How to Play with This Book

This playbook is meant to be read consecutively. Each of the sections creates a foundation to build and evolve into the next. This book is interactive: write in it, scribble, doodle and draw. It is your journal to self-reflect, to play, and explore. Set time aside each week and take it slow. Form a book club and explore with other women. We share our ideas for that at the end of the book. Join our Hot Pink YOUniversity Facebook page and subscribe to our newsletter at www.hotpinkyou.com. We share exciting gatherings, blogs that inform and interactive ways to join our Hot Pink Tribe.

If this book really moves you to take an even deeper exploration of self, let us know. We would love to hear from you.

And, we invite women who are curious to live out loud to work with us on a committed level through our Woman on Fire Program or to travel with us on one of our immersion trips all over the world.

The Four Elements of Living on Fire!

We have created the four elements of becoming the best and brightest you: From the first element, "Put On *Your* Hot Pink Big Girl Panties"; to the second element, "Hot and Juicy, 'I'll Have What She's Having.'" And then moving into the third element, "Burn, Baby, Burn". The final element is "Be a Firestarter–Sparking Others." Each woman's journey will be unique. Hot Pink YOUniversity will be that tribe you can plug into as you start your journey to an incredible and radiant life of Passion, Purpose and Play.

Element I: Put on *Your* Hot Pink Big Girl Panties

It's time to put on *"Your* Hot Pink Big Girl Panties." We will have you doing some serious soul searching and eradication of beliefs that hold you back. This element will set the foundation for all the work that is to come in the weeks and months ahead. It will create a safe and powerful container for you to bust forward and explore the following:

- Panty Raid!
- It's My Hot Pink Baggage and I Claim It!
- Hot Pink Money Love
- The Science of Forgiveness
- The Art of Giving and Receiving

Element II: Hot & Juicy…"I'll Have What She's Having"

Remember the scene from *When Harry Met Sally*? Meg Ryan fakes the orgasm in the cafe that inspires the famous line, "I'll Have What She is Having." This element is all about being "Hot and Juicy" and will focus on all of your desires. It will give you permission you may be waiting for to go out and get what you *want* in life. This element will be the driving force for you to move forward energetically, igniting you to get the life you want to wake up to each and every morning.

- Want and More Are Not Dirty Words
- Pleasure 101
- "Rosetta Stone" for the Hot Pink Tongue
- Hot Pink Travel
- Body Beautiful

Element III: Burn, Baby, Burn!

"Burn, Baby, Burn" will further focus you on action. Your role in *your* life is not as a bystander, but an active participant going out and getting what you want and need. The tools we share will be the match that ignites that already smoldering ember within you. This element is all about combustion! We'll dive into:

Introduction

- Manifesting Big Dreams and Attracting *Your* Desires!
- Getting Out of *Your* Comfort Zone & Jumping into *Your* Flame
- Creating Live Out Loud Moments
- Radical Self-Love
- Power of Play

Element IV: Be A Firestarter—Sparking Others

A Firestarter is a woman, who, once she has got this all figured out…or, at least a piece of it, she then shares that knowledge with another sister-friend. Hot Pink YOUniversity works with women to mentor and guide other women along the way. Through stories and guidance, through listening and calling each other out when needed, we encourage others to become Firestarters. When we hold onto that knowledge and keep it for ourselves, it denies access to other women and to our world. Hot Pink women spark others to be the very best we each can be. We start fires in other women and fan it to a full flame.

- The Art and Science of Hot Pink Relationships
- The Vibe of the Hot Pink Tribe
- Living YOUr Hot Pink Purpose

Element I: Put On *Your* Hot Pink Big Girl Panties!

It is time ladies . . . .
time to **Put On** *Your* **Hot Pink Big Girl Panties**
and move out into the world with renewed power.

It is time to take back *Your* life, to take 100% complete ownership over where you are and where you want to be. No more excuses, no more handing the keys of your Hot Pink car over to someone else and no more sitting in the passenger seat of

Your life. Now, *You* hold the keys and *You* are in the driver's seat. As you are reading this, if you want to blast some empowering chick tunes, get up and dance around the room, *Go For It!* We will be joining you in this dance of passion, pleasure and play…because it is *Your* time!

IT IS A PANTY RAID!

You read it right! It's a self-directed raiding of **Your** panties! It's time to open those drawers and take a peek at what's inside…You get to guide this raid, no one else. Leave the beautiful lacy panties that make you feel feminine and sexy, get rid of the grubby, ripped up, holey, "but they're comfortable" panties. We are replacing these with kicked up-on fire-hot pink panties. You will create limitless ways of thinking, doing and being. We will teach you how to take bold stands for what you want. Make some room. It is time to live out loud.

It is a raid on your thoughts, beliefs, and actions that have been holding you back in life. A raid on self-imposed roadblocks and fears that are getting in your way to living a life you desire. The first step is to clear the old to make room for the new! Everything you believed about yourself, others, and the world is up for the raid. No holding back!

We often move through life on autopilot, not much in intrapersonal examinations of our inner world. *Of course when would we have time to do otherwise?* Yes, it is true, examining life and our inner working takes time. *Isn't it selfish to spend so much time looking at me? I mean, I have others to take care of?* Hello, sister friend! If the plane is going down, the pilot says to put your mask on first before helping the person next to you. It is not selfish to spend time on yourself. When you finally fill your glass up, the overflow from that can then go to others. Without a full glass, you've got nothing! Nothing to give, nothing to offer. Self-care sometimes feels selfish. This is a belief that puts limitations on our lives. It's time to raid that one to make room for something better! We move through life with certain themes that play out over and over and over and over…you get the point. By being more aware of these themes, how they play out in the everyday, and raiding them from our lives, we actually have more time. More time to enjoy, to breath and to care for others as we choose and desire, instead of out of obligation and resentment. It is time to take stock of the themes that cause a major reaction for you and hold you back from seeking the truth.

> *It wasn't until I was halfway done with my run today that I finally figured out why I became so pissed off about a situation the night before. I reacted, or more to the point overreacted, to a fairly typical situation with intensity that embarrassed me. I shot off a few abrupt emails. I felt like crying. I spoke poorly about the person I was mad at, all because I am part of a group traveling in a few weeks and was left out of the email loop, missing a call with the group to connect and get basic travel questions answered. I felt indignant that I also was paying the same amount of money as everyone else and, darn it, deserved to be in the loop! What this situation did was tap into a fundamental need I had/have to be in the loop. Being left out has been a recurrent theme in my life. My sister and my older cousin often left me out. Even another cousin who was my age and three years younger than my sister, preferred her over me. My cousin and I were best friends growing up; but, when it came to a choice to hangout, to play with, even to stand up in her wedding she chose my sister! I was left out. Often shy in grade school—left out. Middle child in my family—left out. Over and over again this became my belief about myself and my trigger to get royally pissed off! In my anger I found power over that vulnerable and painful feeling. I threw rocks at them, I spit and cried, I made fun of them. Ha! You reject me. I reject and hurt you. Translate to adult world. I get pissed off. I throw emails at them, I pout and talk behind their backs. Yada, yada, yada!* ~**The Voice of Christie**

Recurrent Themes

So, here is the juicy part: if we do not dig deep and debunk and dispel those themes they will keep coming up for us and we will react irrationally with automatic thoughts triggering in our head like fireworks on the fourth of July. It brings our energy down or in a direction far of four authentic path. These themes make us believe people are out to get us, to hurt us, to make us feel _____ (fill in the blank with your theme!)

Really?

As if this woman in charge of the trip schemed up a plan to intentionally leave Christie off the email loop. Because she wants to what? Make her feel bad? Make her not want to go? Make her not be or feel included? Our crazy making minds convince us!

Hot Pink Activity 1: Personal Panty Raid!

We want you to take a moment to think about your past. Chunk it out on a piece of paper: 0-12, teen years, young adult, then each decade, twenties, thirties, forties, fifities, sixties, seventies, eighties, nineties. Leave enough space for each decade. Like the stories from the women of Hot PinkYOUniversity, your reality is created out of the stories of your past. Unless you do some work looking at those stories and the themes you have made your reality, you will continue to do the same things expecting different results.

- Who were the people who influenced you? Positively and negatively?
- What were some positive memories and some negative memories?
- What life changing moments did you experience in those chunks of time?
- What were some of your stepping stones in life? What were the beginnings and endings?
- What were your relationships like with your family and your friends?

Take a moment and just ooze on to the paper. Read over what you wrote to yourself and to a trusted friend. What themes do you see emerging? Typical themes include: abandonment and rejection beliefs, mistrust/trust beliefs, feeling left out or a misfit, needing a relationship to feel like you are complete, entitled to things more than others, resentments, that it is not okay to be vulnerable, that somehow something is wrong with you, that you are no good, a failure, that you must be perfect, that it not okay to cry or have emotions, that your needs are not important, that you must fit inside this box here, your thoughts are crazy, you are worthless.

Alongside these negative and limiting beliefs, can be some positive and growth enhancing beliefs. As humans we are wired to immediately encode the negative into our memories within nanoseconds. However, the positive beliefs, happy memories and thoughts can take upwards of twenty seconds or more to encode into our belief system. So, as a kid or young adult, the negative can take a strong hold. If we do not create or develop conditions that will make a fire in our lives burn, like a clearing with fuel and oxygen, the old stuff will snuff out and douse the smoldering ember. Our adult experiences perpetuate and solidify that faulty belief system. It became even deeper and more a survival or habit skill than the reality. The first stage of creating change is awareness of our faulty belief system. Just by doing this activity you are making that commitment to yourself. "*No More*!" You are creating room in your life for more passion, purpose and play!

> "If you do not live the life you believe,
> you will soon believe the life you live."
> ~Adapted from Achbishop Fulton J. Sheen

The messages we grew up with shaped us from that open, white canvas at birth into the women we have become today and can limit the life we hope to have and the person we strive to be.

Old Limiting Beliefs:

- Don't shine too bright, take up too much space, stand out too much.
- Girls should know their place.
- Work your hardest to save for retirement.
- If you do everything the right way, nothing bad will happen.
- You're getting too big for your britches.
- Good girls don't show off, don't question things, behave.
- You can't afford it.

- ✦ You'll never be able to do that.
- ✦ Who the hell do you think you are?

These limiting beliefs become embedded into our thought patterns. We can carry the previous generations issues and beliefs into our own life if we are unaware and lack self-reflections. Science backs this up through epigenetic research. It is our job to say, "*Stop*! *Enough*!". We all entered this world as beautiful babies. We smiled, we laughed, we played, we ate, we slept and we pooped. We were perfect *Love*.

Limiting beliefs can be like capturing a handful of fireflies on a warm, summer evening. We place them in a jar with the lid on and expect them to live through the night. Limiting beliefs snuff out our spark, our right to shine, to burn, to live from within our fire.

Now is the time to develop new and positive beliefs that create an environment conducive for our fire to ignite, to breathe in oxygen, to grow into a raging and beautiful flame.

New Limitless Beliefs:

- ✦ Anything is possible
- ✦ Dream Big
- ✦ Shine bright
- ✦ Be You!
- ✦ You deserve it
- ✦ *You* are enough
- ✦ Pleasure is essential
- ✦ Be bigger than your britches!
- ✦ Your body is a wonderland
- ✦ Can't is a choice
- ✦ Speak *Your* truth
- ✦ I want more!
- ✦ I will, I am, I do!
- ✦ Go for it!

It is a Panty Raid!

Hot Pink Activity 2: Igniting Limitless Beliefs

Circle those words that move you.

Living in my fire, I am a _____ kind of woman:

Luscious	Beautiful	Delicious	Full	Wise
Passionate	Bodacious	Deep	Mighty	Succulent
Joyful	Open	Brilliant	Feminine	Powerful
Juicy	Spiritual	Thong wearing	Sassy	Whimsical
Divine	Masculine	Extraordinary	Sweet	Playful
Courageous	Soulful	Graceful	Happy	Proud
Glorious	Rockin'	Free	Healthy	Grateful
Expansive	Loud	Luminous	Earthy	Sensual
Flirtatious	Raw	Real	Strong	Sexy
Musical	Majestic	Peaceful	Magical	Wild
Awesome	Bold	Pleasure-seeking	Spirit-filled	
Sharing my love Naughty;)	Relaxed	Creative	Geeky	
Silly	Curious	Unapologetic	Artistic	Naked
Deep	Questioning	Radiant	Smart	Bawdy
	Caring	Funny	Articulate	Funky
See, Taste, Touch and Feel		Too big for my britches		
Quiet when I want to be		Downtown Dancing Queen		
Speaking my Truth				

Soul Cleansing:

It's time to cut the crap and quit the shit! Drop the negative thinking. Drop the baggage in your life. Stop defining who you are by what you've been through and what's been done to you. Events shape you but they do not define who you.

> "Things don't happen to you—They happen for you."
> ~Michael Hyatt

We choose to take certain paths in our lives because of our belief system. We may choose to be in relationships that may not be the best for us. We may choose to continue relationships with our families, friends, lovers and colleagues that lack boundaries. We may stifle the life we dreamed about as a young woman. We become caretakers of others and lose caring for ourselves. We fix, protect, rescue and yes, even sometimes, control. We hold on to grudges and become someone we don't want to be and maybe even, don't like.

Hot Pink Activity 3: Hot Pink Relationship Boundaries

- What are the toxic and most difficult relationships in your life right now?
- What relationship would you like to have with that person instead?
- Is that person **willing and able** to be in that type of relationship with you?
- If so, what needs to happen on your end? If not, what needs to change?
- Check in with *You*. When you are feeling that intensity in the overreaction, ask yourself if this is tapping into any childhood themes you are dealing with that are now playing out in the adult arena. If *yes*, recognize it is what it is and that there is no validity to that belief, other than that which you give it. If *no*, what about this current situation is causing the intensity then? Is it a rational concern or an argument to have? What is in your control with the current situation and what is not (*Note: What is not within your control is always a longer list).

A healthy relationship with yourself is:

- One that allows you to have a need and to ask it to be filled
- One that gives you permission to love yourself, all your parts, the good, the bad, the ugly

It is a Panty Raid!

- One that is lived solely about and for you, not for others
- One that makes you feel in your power
- One that supports your authentic self

IT'S MY HOT PINK BAGGAGE AND I CLAIM IT!

"If you own this story, you get to write the ending."
~Brene Brown

Ok, let us start by saying that we are talking all things in the realm of personal responsibility and ownership here…for the good, the bad and everything in between. So, **"hot pink baggage,"** as we talk about it, is the good and the bad stuff alike! It would be expected that here is where we say how it is easy to acknowledge and enjoy our good, warm, fuzzy, success stuff; but, oh so hard to deal with the yucky, painful, shit sandwich stuff; however, we won't be saying that. We won't because we have seen in ourselves and the many women we have spent time with through the years that it is actually equally difficult, if not more so, for us to acknowledge, honor, share and own our good stuff! Part of putting on our big girl hot pink panties is learning how to do just that! We will walk you through ways to take on, learn from and release the bad stuff to make way for how to let go and allow for the real hot pink you to shine through. We know this is very important work to do but we won't linger long here. We have all probably lingered here too long. We get stuck here. We read, attend workshops, journal, and talk about the bad stuff. We look for what will fix it, change it, take it away. We believe that if we work real hard on the bad stuff then the good stuff will organically occur. Not so! We need to grow the hot, juicy, good stuff right along with releasing the crap.

When we talk about personal responsibility and ownership we are referring to the claiming of all your stuff. The declaration of your life experiences, choices, beliefs, body, mind, emotions and relationships as your own. This is where you work on acceptance and how to honor the good, the bad and everything in between as part of your very own journey in this life. When you do that you can then move on to resolve, accept and let go of the things that are not good for you. The things you do not want. It also includes the things you have already learned and no longer need or want. This is what we want you to do with the hard, bad, shit sandwich stuff. We know, easier said than done but believe us it is well worth the work! Remember us sharing the great quote, **"Things don't happen *to* you, they happen *for* you."** That sums it up! How will you use your stuff to learn something about yourself and about others?

Another great quote that Ann coined years ago in reference to the hard, painful, traumatic stuff we experience in life works well to remind us too:

> "It gets you or you get it!"
> ~Ann Murgatroyd-Soe

A Hot Pink woman takes responsibility for herself and owns who she is in this life!!

As therapists and in our own personal lives, we have dealt with all this and know that if we don't come from a place of our strengths then it is pretty hard to move out of old patterns and make changes. So we encourage you to do some shit sandwich work but don't stay long at that buffet! We will challenge you to really lean in to the good stuff. This is where we set the stage for you to really grow, ignite your passions, burn bright and spread the spark to others. This will be the base from which you become a turned on woman who will turn on the YOUniverse!

Responsibility and ownership are not sexy words. They don't conjure much in the way of excitement. They aren't juicy or succulent and often hold the weight of all our have to-, should do, must do- thinking and feeling. We are going to change that.

We are going to make the terms *personal responsibility* and *ownership* Hot Pink!

> ### Hot Pink Activity 4:
> ### Hot Pink *Responsibility* and *Ownership*
>
> Take a few moments to do an association. When you think of the word responsibility, what comes to mind?
>
> Look over your list.
>
> How many of these words get your juices flowing?
> How many are about things that bring you joy? Pleasure?
> How many even have to do with you personally?
> Here is an interesting way to think of the word responsibility:
>
> *"Response-ability": the ability of a person to respond to the various challenges and circumstances of life."*
> ~Dr. Frank Thomas
>
> We like to play creatively with words and like when others do too… in a way that changes it and opens us to new ways of thinking and doing. Now when you think of "response-ability" what words come to mind?
>
> What is the difference in your lists?
> How did the words change with this new perception of the word?
> Try this: List what it is that you want to have the ability to respond to more freely, openly, and joyfully?
>
> Think of at least three things you can do to make these happen in your life. Go do it!

> ### Hot Pink Activity 5: Self-love Jar
>
> Get a glass jar with cover and decorate it anyway you choose…a simple ribbon or decoupage it full of images you love. Each time you have a feel good, hot pink moment, experience, accomplishment write it on a slip of paper and put it in the jar. At 6 months and then again ta year open the jar and read all the good stuff you have manifested in your life. You can go to the jar during the tough times when you are dealt a shit sandwich too and just read a few to regain perspective and reignite.

So, you have your Hot Pink Baggage and you claim it! Now we want you to let go of the bad stuff but not before you have learned all that you want and need from it! You are on your way to being a Hot Pink Firestarter!

The remainder of Element I: Put on Your Hot Pink Big Girl Panties will address some core issues that come up frequently in our work with women in our playshops, events, retreats, travel and coaching. These core issues include: money, forgiveness and receiving. They are essential issues before we move into our Element II.

Many women live from a mindset of scarcity, not enough time, not enough money, and not enough _____, fill in the blank with your favorite scarcity. This scarcity mindset is often an illusion or habitual way of thinking that has never been addressed. Women in this mindset wake each morning with thoughts like: "I didn't get enough sleep", "I won't have enough time to get to work", or "there is never enough money". This mindset limits our potential for experiences and for out of the box ways of living. Our life goals become stunted. Remember as a kid when the days seemed longer, you played for what felt like forever and then collapsed into bed each night. There weren't any more hours in the day then, just an expansion of time created by your mindset as a kid. As an adult, our over-stacked to do lists and overscheduled lives, create the perspective of scarcity. Our habits like Facebook surfing and television watching as well as not being in the moment, further perpetuate this way of thinking. We create scarcity around money by avoiding looking at our finances, overspending, or thinking we cannot create a greater flow of income.

HOT PINK MONEY LOVE

Money, not everyone's favorite topic. It seems to elicit extremes, extreme love and desire and greed, to extreme hate and loathing and martyrdom. Women, in recent history, have not had a great relationship with money. Often it was controlled by others, inaccessible, and a distant concept. As we work with women in Hot Pink YOUniversity, we strive to heal that relationship with money and to foster a new relationship with it all together. One that sustains and makes you feel secure. One that creates pleasurable experiences. One that makes you feel strong and powerful.

Hot Pink Activity 6: Money Relationship

If you had to describe your relationship with money right now, what would it be? Pick one below or create your own...maybe it is a combination of a few, or changes from day to day, paycheck to paycheck.

My current relationship with money is:

Friend	Lover	Father	Mother	Distant relative
Enemy	Abusive Boyfriend		Cousin	Brut
Bastard	Best friend	Girlfriend	Controlling Partner	
Unfair Parent				

Our relationship with money is often shaped early on. From the earliest of memories, what do you remember about money?

How was money handled/managed/mismanaged in your family?

> Take a dollar bill and place it in your hand. What kind of emotions do you have about money? What if that dollar were $1,000 or $10,000?
>
> | Scarcity | Avoidance | Fear | Anger | Control | Victim |
> |---|---|---|---|---|---|
> | Guilt | Shame | Desire to "hoard" | | Blame | Resentment |

New money mindsets can have the following feelings when we hold money in our hands. Feelings like: freedom, giving, abundance, security, ease, fun, creativity, gifts, choices, independence, dreams, expansion, learning

When you heal your relationship with money, you put money back into the place it belongs. It is energy. And any consuming or selling is just an exchange of that energy. You buy a home and take out a loan, you are now energetically tied to the bank each and every time your mortgage is due. If your home was $150,000, you never actually had the bank come to you with a case holding $150,000 in actual cash. You signed your name and agreed to the terms and the energy of those terms. When you get your paycheck, your employer does not actually come to your desk and start counting the bills out. You get a piece of paper that contains an energy and attach some feeling or worth to the numbers that you see and the numbers it creates, or does not create in your bank account. Very little of our day is spent actually holding the money notes. Yet, so much of our day has thoughts around money.

Here are some core Hot Pink beliefs about money:

- **Whatever your relationship is with money, make it a positive one.** It is necessary to live. It has been around forever in one form or another, even in the times of bartering, it was energy of some kind being exchanged.

Goats=money, beads=money, furs=money. You get our point.
- **Money in the Right Hands Can Do Amazing Things!** And, we believe the shift towards the feminine in healing the world also means a shift in the feminine having greater access and caretaking of money. Imagine what feminine energy might do with money? In healing our relationship with money, we open a container for the flow of money into our lives.
- **What you attend to grows.** When was the last time you balanced your account or made and stuck to a budget, a plan? When was the last time you knew the exact flow of in and out. Often, when we have a negative relationship with money, we ignore and avoid or get angry. If money becomes your friend, your lover, and you ignored it and didn't take the time to get to know it, what would happen to that relationship?
- **Having money does not make you greedy, rich, snobby.** It makes you abundant, potentially giving. It makes you secure and independent. It creates an opening to further achieve, grow and reach.

Hot Pink Activity 7: Money Must Do's

Money Mondays. Every Monday, look at your money. Open your online account, check your transactions, write your checks, be aware of the in and the out flow of money. Did we say every Monday? *Yes!*

- Name the relationship you desire to have with money:
- Calculate the most you have ever made in a month:
- Calculate what you would like to make a month:
- Calculate an amount that you could have in a month and add in some juicy pleasurable things:
- Calculate an obscene amount of money a month:

> Playing with these numbers helps us grow our awareness of money and our relationship with money. It also helps us to frame our desires and dreams that may only be attainable through money. Create some new and healthy beliefs around money and write them:

Listen to Hot Pink YOUniversity's two part blogtalk radio program on money:

http://www.blogtalkradio.com/hotpinkyou/2014/08/22/financing-your-passions-getting-clear-on-your-money-with-hot-pink-youniversity

http://www.blogtalkradio.com/hotpinkyou/2014/09/08/part-two-financing-your-passions-hot-pink-youniversity-money-talk

I was sitting around the table with some Hot Pink sister friends when the topic of money came up in the conversation. One of my friends said to me, "I know you don't feel the same pressures about money that we do." It hits me hard and a clear WTF calls out in my head. I pause just a moment to question myself and whether I am going to say anything. This is a "Firestarter" moment for me and I know it. Is it important enough to me to speak up? Am I gonna be hot pink or stay quiet and then deal with the inevitable rehashing in my own mind that will come later after the conversation is done and we have all packed up and headed home? Hell yea, it resonated so quickly and loudly in me that I had to speak up.

"What do you mean when you say that I don't have pressure about money?" Game on. I am speaking up in honor of my emotions. I feel that burst of strength and energy that comes from a heightened state of interaction. But I also feel the slightest bit of fear and definite discomfort. I don't like confrontation. Don't like it at all although I respect it as a hallmark of healthy communication in

relationships. This is one of my soul sistas...if I can't with her then with who the hell will I ever be able to? Funny thing too, I am very capable of assertive confrontation in many areas of my life, with my business partner, with my psychotherapy clients, with my employees, my peers. In my personal relationships, not so much! I all too often just retreat in my mind to whatever not so good feeling the situation evoked and "suck it up" which tends to make it hard to let it go! Yea, I then carry it around and bring it out in my thoughts every so often just to feel shitty, hurt, pissed, confused all over again. Don't want to cause a problem, rock the boat, hurt someone's feelings, have someone upset with me! Not very hot pink and not gonna do it this time. I want to really talk to her about this and express my feelings as well as clarify my reality.

"Well, you have resources that we don't. I mean I remember you saying that if anything ever happened your families would help you out and you have all that land. Sometimes we are just down to the wire with money". *Wow...I am thinking. I have just had a window into a way I am perceived by one of my closest friends. Somehow she believes that I am "set" financially although all arrows would point to multiple life changes in the last few years saying otherwise. Why does she feel I am somehow in a more secure socioeconomic circumstance than she and my other soul sista? Seems to me we are all on similar ground in this area yet she has me leaps and bounds ahead in the money game! What about my presence gives this impression to someone who knows me so well? Why the hell does it even bother me that she would think it?*

"I don't have those resources today. My parents are gone. I am divorced...I don't have a husband or in-laws there for me now, that land isn't mine personally and it isn't cash available to me in the event of a need. It's just me. I am all on my own here". *She nods and I feel some relief but also the need to push forward a bit.*

"I only have my income now and I am all on my own financially for everything. I see that balance in my checking and get that feeling. Things get tight for me too". Again, I am wondering how I give off such a different impression to her? I feel I am pretty real and open. I mean, I don't have detailed conversations about finances but I also don't behave or live in a way that would speak of "affluence"…do I? Here I go, now I am pulling this all in as if it were my responsibility that she holds this perception. This is what I do, assume it must be something about me or what I do that "causes" the situation. I begin to self-doubt, personalize, and worry.

"I didn't know all that, maybe you just don't get as affected by it all then, maybe you are just good at hiding it". Again I am wondering why I am being put in such a different category? Although, she is right, I don't seem to be. Now, I am searching, reflecting and this is much better than personalizing or doubting for sure! The word 'hiding' isn't sitting well with me though.

"You know, I am affected and it is my reality too but I don't let myself worry very much about money anymore. I had money once and worried often what if we didn't have it. All those fears came true. My husband's companies sold, shut down, jobs lost. We never really recovered from all that. The money and all that was gone. Now I am a divorcee with a son in college. I had it and I lost it so I am not afraid of it anymore. I mindfully choose not to worry about money". Again, she nods and smiles. It felt good to speak up. It lead to a great conversation with my hot pink sisters about money, fear, prosperity, fear, financial independence, fear, abundance, fear. Not easy topics for women to explore or share about but we did. It felt great. It was beautiful. We each owned some shit, called out what didn't fit for us personally and professionally, and held each other up in where we were each at when it came to money. **~The Voice of Ann**

Hot Pink Money Love

This story illustrates what an emotional topic money can be for women. The assumptions we make about others and money can shape our friendships. Ann has made the choice to not worry about money, to not have a mindset of scarcity or lack. It creates a sense of well-being, to have the relationship with money be a hot pink partnership.

THE SCIENCE OF FORGIVENESS

Forgiveness is a vital perspective shift needed in order to move forward beyond limitations and into our authentic lives. Warren Buffet was interviewed on CBS Sunday Morning. One of the wealthiest people in America, he was not born into his wealth, he created it. And now, at eighty two he is giving a lot of it away. What does he attribute to his success? When interviewed he said that it all began in the womb—with luck. He was born a white male in the 1930s, not another race, not female. Now, when he says this, he is not bashing the other alternatives. He is clearly honoring and respecting and acknowledging his luck. It all starts in the womb. By luck, our mother takes good care of her body while we are bathing in the warm amniotic fluid provided by our momma. By luck we are born into a set of circumstances that are healthy. That our environment is stable and loving with all the right messages to go out into the world and hold our head high with self-confidence and self-love. However, not many of us start out with such luck or grace. We begin the battle towards self-acceptance and self-love very early on.

So, how do we clear this negative start to life? This poor fate? These shit sandwiches. Maybe it was the verbal abuse you endured as a kid, or being told you're too fat, too sensitive, too _____(fill in the blank). Or maybe you received the best kind of love your caretakers could give you, but there were mixed messages intertwined in those loving messages and you just never felt like you measured up. Or, you felt your brother was loved more than you. Or, your parents worked so damn hard to create a good life, but the message became, "my parents job is more important than I am". Whatever your beginnings were, it is now time to take control over those messages and release the control they have over you to be the best you that you can be.

Shayla Logan is one of the most positive outlook people we know. Despite having an extremely difficult childhood and health struggles along the way, she exudes the desire to reframe shit sandwiches in life, create her own perceptions and live in a positive world. In a Facebook post in 2011, she wrote:

> "Forgiveness is never about the other person. Someone hurts us and then we hurt ourselves by bringing up the issue in our minds and hearts over and over again, reigniting that pain. Forgiveness is about claiming your power and putting an end to the damage you're doing to yourself by consciously choosing to release your past." ~Shayla Logan

When we feel victimized we often seek revenge, make the other person feel bad, as bad as we possibly feel, we hold onto our grudges and stay firmly planted in our victim stories. It is kind of like staying stuck in a bad country song, "somebody done me wrong," way of thinking. If we are to break free of these chains of grudge holding and move into our true light, we need to learn the science of forgiveness.

Take a moment to think of those people in your life now and from the past, that you have been holding anger and resentment over. The action might have been as minimal as saying something or doing something hurtful to as big as causing considerable physical and emotional pain. It could be as big as causing a life-changing moment for you. The kind of moment that changed the direction you were heading. We have worked with some people in life facing some pretty horrendous pains. The loss of a loved one due to an accident, the loss of a job, the end to a relationship…how do we get beyond some of these deep losses and changes we did not choose?

"Forgiveness…it's a big word. I have struggled with it. I have learned it doesn't mean turning a cheek or minimizing. It means truly leaning into it all and working through it. It means taking stock in what was done to you, what part you might have played, if any and how you have allowed it to affect you. I have already shared in my story that my father-my rock, my mentor, my friend was killed in a car accident and my mother left horribly injured and widowed. They were hit by a man that barreled across three lanes of traffic in broad daylight on a wide open, no obstruction of view highway intersection on a sunny April afternoon. (can you hear my pain and struggle here?) I can tell you that I have felt every conceivable emotion and thought every terrible thought about this man and what he did to my family. I can also tell you that I spent a lot of time in healing and that it wasn't always done in a neat, orderly, understandable and productive way. Sometimes it was horrible, dark, ugly, angry, hopeless, broken, all-consuming, devastating swallow me up kind of pain. I eventually began to shift my language, to understand that, as humans, we are imperfect, that accidents do happen with terrible outcomes and that this man certainly didn't intend to kill my father and that he and his family will live with their own painful awareness and impact for the rest of their lives too. He was not drinking, he was not speeding, he was plainly said, not watching, waiting, focusing clearly enough to know that he did not have the time or space to make it across traffic or to see my father's truck approaching. I began to open myself to understanding the bigger picture, the very nature of human lives…the beginnings and endings and the life that happens in between. I realized that I was, in my own healing journey forgiving this man for the seemingly unforgiveable irresponsibility he showed that day behind the wheel. I challenged myself to consider the times in the past that I may have lost focus, reached for the radio tuning knob, looked at my passenger in conversation or laughter and not been my most

clear, responsible, eyes wide open self behind the wheel. It wasn't easy to do but I did know the truth, accidents do happen and lives are forever changed in an instant. I worked to heal my heart in part by recognizing that it I was forever changed and it would get me or I would get it! I let go of the victim thinking, I spent years in the survivor thinking in order to just make it and take care of my life and loved ones. Eventually, I was ready to move in to thriving. I was changed. I realized how important it is to live every minute of life to the fullest. A fire was lit by my forgiveness and I was ready to combust. I made many huge life changes to create a passion filled life. I opened my own mental health clinic, never to be an employee again. I set clear boundaries in my closest relationships, I said yes to my desire to travel, to buy that fast, hot car, I left a marriage that did not meet my needs or compliment my passions, I let go of the tight Momma grip I had on my son as he faced his own challenges in creating his young adult life. I stopped taking responsibility for others in my life. I said good-by and I wish you well to some friendships that were unbalanced and not supporting me in my greatest good. Forgiveness gave me that ability to start living again and it has made all the difference."
~The Voice of Ann

Forgiveness allows us to release painful feelings that make it hard to move forward into light, free up energy for really good stuff, stand in the present and look to the future, not be owned by the past. Forgiveness is a gift we give to ourselves because the only person that is hurt by not forgiving is our own true spirit.

"When my son was little, we often read The Littlest Angel by Charles Tazwell, it is a book about a soul coming down to earth in this lifetime and dimming their light so much as to do harm to the other little soul. That the first soul's dimming is a sacrificial gift to this other soul so that he may do his part on her earthly journey to live and learn the valuable lesson on forgiveness. But, in the

end he wants her to remember that he is still light, that he is recognizable and still just a soul much like herself."
~The Voice of Christie

There are lessons to be learned in our darkest moments, like what we have already stated previously,

"Things don't happen to you, they happen for you."
~Michael Hyatt

Hot Pink Activity 8a: Victim Letter

Make a list of those you feel who have wronged you. Next, choose one person from your list to whom you will write a letter. This **first letter** in a series of three is your victim letter, like the country song, what wrong has somebody done to you? what feelings do you have about that person—hate? disgust? fear? anger? vent it all out in this unsent letter to this person, how it has impacted your life in a negative way, how it has changed you and why you are angry about that change. Reread that letter to yourself. Though this person is the designated recipient of this letter, the benefit of writing it is for you, vent out the shame and guilt feelings you have.

Hot Pink Activity 8b: I Forgive You Letter

The **second letter** to do when you are ready is the "I forgive" letter. This is a really important and difficult step in the process. What you are writing here is the I forgive you for... (to the person who has wronged you) included in this letter, and this might be a difficult step- I forgive myself for....This trips us up sometimes and is a necessary thought process in the movement towards forgiveness. We have worked with women in therapy after an awful divorce following the affair her husband had. In her process of writing this letter, some of the women are stumped, "What the hell do I need forgiving for? I am not the one that had the affair!" In these moments, we invite women to share some thoughts on that and here is what generally comes out for them:

"I forgive myself for holding onto this pain and needing to be a victim in my story. I forgive myself for the wrongs and shortcomings that contributed to our negative marital environment in the first place. I realize that affairs don't happen in happy and content marriages. I forgive myself for this hate I feel. I forgive myself for being so fucking needy right now, for feeling broken beyond repair, for feeling like life will never get better. I forgive myself for not trusting my ability to meet a man, to choose a man, to trust my judgment. I forgive me and I love me for all my imperfections. "

By forgiving ourselves we move into our authentic life and can radiate more peacefully and more full of love.

> ### Hot Pink Activity 8c: Gratitude Letter
>
> The **third letter** is the final step in the forgiveness process and it is the gratitude or thank you letter. *I thank you for*_____ Here you write are the lessons that you learned about life, about yourself, your own inner strength, how you want to move through the world. We tend to focus on the negatives in life and it takes real effort to move in this direction, but so important for our emotional and spiritual growth.
>
> *"I have learned that I have such abundant strength. That things happen, bad and terrible things, but that I must go on. I have learned that I can go on in great joy and gratitude for what I have. I have learned that what people think doesn't matter nearly as much as what I think. I have learned that I deserve great love and light in life. These are lessons I never would have learned without the hurt that you caused me by your actions. I have grown into this beautiful woman of power and greater compassion and I thank you for your contribution in that growth."*

Again, these letters are for you, are about you and benefit you. They do not need to be sent to the other person unless you feel so compelled to do so. The purpose of the three letter process is to release, reflect, and gain insight for new growth. It is clearing the "shit sandwiches" from your life so that you can prepare to set the stage for your fire!

> "It has been said, 'Time heals all wounds.' I do not agree. The wounds remain. In time, the mind, protecting its sanity, covers them with scar tissue and the pain lessens. But it is never gone." ~Rose Kennedy

Okay, this is one way to look at things. And, it is true, time does heal and the memories may never be gone; but, what if we made our peace with the past and chose to stay mindfully in the present, looking towards what we do have control over and that is the future. What if we radically forgave the past and decided to take what lessons it had to offer to us? Instead of being the *victim or survivor* of our story, we could be heroic thriver of our future. Things, sometimes some very bad things, happen for a reason and it is up to us to decide to turn these difficulties into life lessons. By not forgiving the past, we are only hurting ourselves and stopping ourselves from reaching our highest potential. Make peace with your past. Symbolically, write down your victim story and burn it, sending it up to the skies.

> *"I once did something in my life so bad, so unforgiving… even just thinking back to it, makes me shudder and ask myself, "What the hell was I thinking?!" I mean, this behavior was so against my values, my philosophy of life, that it bolted me out of self-love into self-loathing for quite some time…won't even share what it is…that's how bad!"* ~**Hot Pink YOUniversity Firestarter (but, could be any of us!)**

What if the person to forgive is ourselves? We've all done some things in life that when we look back at the video of our lives. It makes us want to block that little chunk out. Or, maybe we react with rationalization or justification to our deed, "Well, he f%#@ing deserved it," "Well, I did that, but what she did was so much worse." or "I wouldn't have done that if…". Wouldn't it be easier to just admit our mistake, ask for forgiveness and move on? The problem sometimes becomes that time heals all wounds—even the wounds we create. People do move on and they do forgive…but, the last person to forgive you is often you.

We hear about forgiveness all the time and how it heals the wounds. It is the bigger thing to do. That when we forgive it is not about the other person, it is a gift we give to ourselves. What if the person who hurts you is ***You***?

In the Christian faith these are sins. In Buddhism the deeds affect your karma. In politics these are skeletons in the closet of life. It does not matter in what context we are interpreting our actions. When we act outside of our concept of self and what is a good life, when we hurt others, it impacts our self-love.

Guilt? Shame?

When we feel guilt and we are not talking about the low self-esteem, self-deprecating comments we often say to ourselves. We are talking about legitimate guilt; as in, "I did this…it is not within what I value or believe in for my life. I made a legitimate mistake." When we feel this kind of guilt it is good. It makes us feel uncomfortable enough in life to change our course and move in another, better direction. Guilt is our moral compass at times.

But, when we feel shame, self-loathing—"I AM that behavior kind of feeling"—we get stuck. We do not change course. We do not forgive our actions as just that, an action. We let it define us, and it dims the fire within so that we are no good to ourselves, others or the planet.

"The only mistake there is, is the one we do not learn from."
~Christie Gause-Bemis

What is your mistake? Your actions? How did it impact you? Impact others?

> *"My mother said to me (my oh so wise teacher in life) "The last person that will forgive you is you…God already has. Imagine the love you feel for your son, is there anything he can do that would cause you to not forgive him." And, honestly, there is not. That is how great our love can be for another! She said, "That is how God feels for you ten thousand fold"* **~The Voice of Christie**

It does not matter what word you use for your divine, your higher power. The love you have for another could be the love you feel for yourself, ten thousand fold. What would it take to forgive yourself? What did you learn from this mistake? What gifts came out of it? Self-forgiveness leads to self-love and grows that ember into a fire inside—so that you may enjoy life and shine that out to others. We don't know about you, but to us, that sounds pretty darn good!

THE ART OF GIVING AND RECEIVING

For most woman, giving is the easy part. We are wired for it neurologically. According to Louann Brizendine, author of T*he Female Brain*, our brains and biology are wired for caretaking. The problem with only giving is we don't ask for what we want and need. We end up feeling resentful. We get so worn out, that in the end, we have nothing left of ourselves to give when we have not balanced giving with our ability to receive. To receive is to fill ourselves back up. The symbol for a woman, the chalice, the perfect receptacle to fill, to receive. Yet, we deny ourselves, don't ask for what we want or need and put the needs of others before our own.

Hot Pink Activity 9: Hot Pink Receiving

What words come to mind when we say, "Receive." Write those down. Write down all the ways you give to others.

The real, raw Hot Pink truth is that if we want to live a life we desire **out loud and on fire**, we *must* learn to **Receive equally to what we Give**. We *must* do two very important things to live a full balanced life at our full potential for being out loud and on fire! First, we must learn to do all those things for ourselves. Go back again and look over that list above on the ways you give and this time write some intention statements. "I will *give* to myself by_____." "I will *care* for myself by_____." The very way you give to others, is what you need to receive for self.

The second and equally important concept is to open ourselves to receiving from others. This means when it is openly offered to you, you accept. And when you need, you ask for what you need!

In order for us to give to others at our highest potential, we must be balanced in our own life and this undoubtedly includes the balancing of self with others, giving and receiving!

> "Until we can receive with an open heart, we're never really giving with an open heart. When we attach judgment to receiving help, we knowingly or unknowingly attach judgment to giving help." ~Brené Brown

Hot Pink YOUniversity Tips for Receiving:

- **Build your tribe**. Support systems are necessary. If we feel unsupported then we often turn to "doing" even more for others, fixing more, solving more problems, supporting others more as a way of feeling productive. It creates even more imbalance and we become "burned out caretakers"
- **Receiving is Feminine Energy**. To receive is at the very core, a feminine energy…we receive in order to create by nature. Like penis to vagina, sperm to egg, child in womb. When we only give and block the receiving, we are literally shutting down our feminine nature.
- **Create Positive Mantras.** Come up with a couple positive phrases that will remind you to receive. *Open, Allow, and Flow* is one of ours and works well. Other examples: " I will say yes, I will accept kindnesses, I will allow myself to receive, I will gift myself, I will ask."
- **Take Compliments!** Don't minimize or negate a compliment. We once heard Jana Stanfield in a concert talk about compliments and she suggested that we not only accept a compliment given, but that we take it one step further and say "Thank you and not only that but…

(insert your own compliment here, I'm also good at cooking)!!" It is also important to linger for a moment or two to truly absorb the power of the compliment. Brain research shows negative events embed in our memory in nanoseconds, almost instantly; but good things have to be mindfully held for up to 20 to 60 seconds for it to imprint and store in our minds.

- **Truly honor/accept a gift.** Because of our messed up thinking, we will negate a gift without even realizing. We are "being nice," when say things like "Oh, you shouldn't have," or "You don't have to do this," "You're too generous." Stop for a second and actually listen to what is said there. These phrases, although not intended to be, are like opening a gift and throwing it back at the giver. It dismisses the beauty of the gesture and takes away from the good feeling the giver has in wanting to gift you.
- **Start small.** Most of us are so out of practice…or never really learned in the first place so starting with little acceptances and asks is easier on us. We can work our way up. Practice and build up to the bigger stuff!
- **Honor the natural balance/cycle of Giving and Receiving.** There is a true cycle here, and interdependence to be functioning at our best. If we give then we must also receive or we are breaking nature's balance and something is gonna give! Usually it is our own health and well-being.
- **Know what you really desire.** So often I hear women say, "I don't even know what I want or need." We get so far removed from gifting ourselves, receiving or asking that we eventually don't even know what we *want more* of. (Remember those are not dirty words and we will cover that more in the next section.) Create a Want More or Desire List. Then list at least one thing you can do to make it happen.

- **Obstacles to receiving?** List them, look for underlying common messages (not worthy, good enough, others will suffer/not get needs met, I will not be needed.) then reframe. Selfish-to self-care. Not worthy-I am enough. Too expensive-I am worth it. It is all about energy exchange and how it flows. If we shut down our own bodies, hearts, souls from receiving then we have interrupted the flow and we will not be able to create, share, and give at our highest greatest good. As with all things, nature seeks balance. Yin/Yang, Male/Female, good/evil, lightness/darkness. As women we are often very imbalanced in the Giving/Receiving realm. Culturally we are taught from childhood the value of giving but rarely are we taught the value and necessity of receiving. This sets us up for imbalance and messes with *Flow*.
- **Ask for what you want.** So often we hear women express disappointment for not getting their needs or desires met by others. When we say, "Did you ask?" We hear that she did not or "If I have to ask, then it is not as meaningful". We ask "Why?" If we ask for our children for some time or our spouses for flowers or a night out, and they respond by doing that, it is just as meaningful, if not more so. We asked and that person responded out of love. And, what if they don't? At least we asserted our needs. Now the rest is on the other person and their actions or inactions define who they are-not who we are.

Open, Allow, Flow! Write these on paper and put them in easily seen places at home and office.

There are Three Types of Receiving:

- **Gifting** yourself
- **Receiving** when given
- **Asking** for what you want /need.

> ### Hot Pink Activity 10: Gift, Receive, & Ask
>
> *Activity*: write each type of receiving at the top of a page of paper. Write for the next couple minutes as many examples of each as you can from your own life.
>
> Examples:
>
> Gift: Buying something special that you desire (a scarf, a class you want to experience, a trip)
>
> Receive: When someone offers you help-take it. A gift-thank them. A favor-enjoy without keeping the score.
>
> Ask: "I miss you and desire to spend time with you." "It would be so nice if you bought me flowers when we go to the market today." "I need you to take this off my to do list and put it on yours."

Author Amanda Owen in her book, *The Power of Receiving: A Revolutionary Approach to Giving Yourself the Life You Want and Deserve* poses the question, "Who is the Giver and who is the Receiver when we look at the relationship between a butterfly and a butterfly bush? They give to each other and receive from each other." Receiving at its very core is nature's way to balance and prosper. This is quantum physics here… string theory…we can't give without receiving and we can't receive without giving!

Element II:
Hot & Juicy…"I'll Have What She's Having!"

Women all over the world and across time have inspired us to live our lives out loud and claim what is ours. It is time to look around and see that the wheel has already been invented by these women of enormous power, grace, beauty and fire. Women like: Oprah Winfrey, Louise Brooks (silent movies in the 1920's), Princess Diana, Madonna, Lady Gaga, Pink, Eleanor Roosevelt, Lucille Ball, Mother Theresa, Marilyn Monroe, Holocaust victim, Anne Frank, Michelle Obama and fifteen-year-old Malala Yousufzai of Pakistan, shot for advocating education for girls. These women and many others are Hot Pink Women, living large and proud lives. These women shine so bright, we want a little of that. It is that famous Meg Ryan moment at the diner in the movie, *When Harry Met Sally* that we seek. When she fakes the orgasm and elicits the desire of the woman at the next table to say, "I'll have what she's having." That orgasmic joy of living a life on fire!

So, how do we get what she is having? With a little more juice, a little more courage, a little more succulence and a lot more passion, pleasure and play. This is about living out loud with no apologies!

You have cleared the shit in life and embraced your true authentic self. The woman standing in the mirror deserves to have it all!

There are broken parts to the Hot Pink Woman. Oh, yes indeed. We choose to acknowledge and love these broken parts. It is what makes us unique and compassionate. It is Wabi Sabi self-love. Wabi Sabi is a Japanese view of accepting one's imperfections and flaws. The revered crack in Japanese pottery that is then filled in with gold, not to hide it, but to celebrate and behold its uniqueness because of the crack. No other pottery can have that same crack. No other woman has your same flaws, your vulnerabilities, your mistakes. *You* are unique and flawed. It is because of those flaws you have grown and blossomed to bring forth this beautiful goddess! A power-filled force to be reckoned with.

Hot and Juicy…"I'll have what she is having!" is all about embracing your body beautiful, creating a safe and succulent sisterhood, gaining confidence, creating limitless beliefs, gaining control over our life, our environment, our money, knowing the true power of our words and how we narrate our "herstory." It is about being okay with wanting, desiring, and having more, clarifying our greatest desires, gratitude for what we have. This is the hot and juicy that we are having at Hot Pink YOUniversity and you can order up for yourself too.

WANT AND MORE: THEY ARE NOT DIRTY WORDS!

They are not words most women feel comfortable with. They are not words women use and surely not words we live by. When we gather women and start to talk about *Want* and *More* we can see and feel the discomfort. Women begin to squirm, furrow their brows, shake their heads stiffen their postures, and are already playing the messages that are so deeply engrained…"It's not about what I want", "I should be happy with what I have" "I am content", "Less is more", "It's not spiritual to want", "I shouldn't expect anything more", "It's been so long, I don't even know what I would want", to name just a few.

Hot Pink Activity 11: Want and More Mindshifts

Journal Prompts

What thoughts came to you when you read the words, *Want* and *More*?
How did those words make you feel?
Where did those beliefs/messages about *Want* and *More* come from?

It's time for that Hot Pink Panty Raid again ladies! Those thoughts and beliefs gotta go! *Want* and *More* are not dirty words! So, why do they feel that way to women? We often hear women say that they are "selfish" words. Selfish by definition is:

adjective: selfish

1. lacking consideration for others; concerned chiefly with one's own personal profit or pleasure.
   "I joined them for selfish reasons" (source: google.com)
   synonyms: egocentric, egotistic, egotistical, egomaniacal, self-centered, self-absorbed, selfobsessed, self-seeking, self-serving, wrapped up in oneself

We have become so externally focused that to even ponder what we *want more* of in our own lives not only seems unattainable, it seems selfish, ungrateful, even wrong. Where did it all start, the ideas that to have *wants* is somehow diametrically opposed to being there for those we love, those who count on us? Surely we *want more* for the ones we love! But for ourselves, not so much. It just doesn't add up when you really take a look at this concept and that is just what we are doing…taking a long hard look and jumping in to our desires!

This is where we open you up to the necessity—yes, the necessity, not luxury of *want* and m*ore* in your life. If you are going to live a life on fire, you gotta go for what you want and desire more of in your life. This is essential to move into our third element, Burn, Baby, Burn! At Hot Pink YOUniversity, here's what we know…

To honor our Wants and to desire More is not selfish.
It is self-care.

Self-care by definition is:

noun: self-care

1. Referring to the actions which contribute to the maintenance of wellbeing, personal health and promoting personal development. It is the actions you take to care for mind, body and spirit.
   "I am practicing good self-care"

Want and More: They Are NOT Dirty Words!

Synonyms: self-sufficient, independent, confident, efficient, self-reliance, strength, power, resilience (source: google.com)

It is part of how we live a life on fire and out loud. It is not an adjective like selfish. It does not describe who we are or create a description of how we are in relation to others. (Although certainly when we come from a place of good self–care, we are much better able to relate to, care for and inspire others). It is about what we do and how we feel from the inside out! It is about unapologetically honoring our own wellbeing and happiness right along and **equal** to that of others.

Want and *More* are words of power, inspiration, wellness, health, healing, wholeness…the list goes on! At Hot Pink YOUniversity, we are redefining *Want* and *More*! We believe these two words need to become a core part of your language and your life. Now that we have invited you to think more positively about the words *Want* and *More*, let's go for it!

Hot Pink Activity 12: Want and More Words

We started a list for you of all sorts of juicy words. Circle those from the list below that call out to you, that you *Want More* of in your life. Please add any of your own as well. You are on your way to creating your own Hot Pink Womanifesto!

I want more…

Pleasure   **POWER**   **Succulence**   Sensuality   **Passion**   *Joy*
Fun   **Gratitude**   **DESIRE**   **Play**   Sex

Bliss Now go back and pick one or two words you circled to do some work on. Write the word at the top of your journal page, then write an intention statement such as "I *want more* _____ in my life." List as many ways you can think of, big and small to create this in your life. This is your action plan!

> Are there words you wanted to choose but did not? Why? What might this mean?
>
> Did you choose those that were most comfortable/easiest to achieve or those that you know will be way out of your comfort zone?

This last activity invites you to think about what you desire, what you want to increase in your life, your deepest longings. If you chose words that felt safer and easier, that is all good too. Go ahead and make it happen for yourself *and* now add one or two that really push you, that make you squirm a bit, that you might even fear and do the same with those! If you chose to really go for it right away and take yourself way out of your comfort zone, that is all good too! If you find yourself struggling and then avoiding your growth in that area, then go back and pick a couple that are easier and go get recharged before you try for the hard ones again!

PLEASURE 101

Pleasure…we have been thinking about it, talking about it, reading about it and embracing it a lot lately. It is a powerful word. It evokes different things at different times to different people. One thing that seems consistent though is that women want it deep down inside but also struggle with having it or allowing the experience of pleasure. We find ourselves drawn more each day to developing and sharing what we call **The Hot Pink Pleasure Principle**. It is a fundamental part of our message at Hot Pink YOUniversity.

So often we seem to have an underlying sense of discomfort, even guilt over the desire for pleasure. We somehow think it is an *occasional luxury* to seek pleasure. We want you to know that it is essential for your health and that of your loved ones, to expect and create pleasure in all areas of your life. We wish to create joy, happiness and pleasure for others but feel guilty to seek it ourselves or even to accept it from others. Pleasure and joy allow you to be balanced and put your best selves out there in the world. If you wish to be your best for those you love, you need to be at your best and pleasure is one of the main self-care ingredients for sure! Imagine what your life would be like if you honored the power of pleasure each day!

Pleasure isn't found in just big, fun, fluffy stuff like vacations, spa days, birthday and other celebrations you know, the stuff we get every so often but not often enough to sustain, balance and grow ourselves. Don't get us wrong. We think those are all important, amazing and necessary too. But in order to live a life from the Pleasure Principle we need the smaller more frequent pleasures as well.

Once you pay attention and mindfully seek pleasure in your daily life you can find it just about anywhere in anything! We actually *look for* pleasures now. It can be the crisp citrus smell in your kitchen just after you clean. The smell of the fall leaves when pruning the shrubs for winter. It comes in the shift from distress to safety and calm in the face of a friend when you have listened and hugged her through a painful situation. We often find it in the energized feeling we each have after a kick ass creative day working on all things Hot Pink YOUniversity!

Our definition of The Pleasure Principle is: to commit not only to giving pleasure but receiving and seeking it from big bold brilliant experiences every so often to smaller yet equally powerful moments in everyday life. We encourage you to gift yourself pleasures big and small. A pleasure filled woman radiates and spreads that message to everyone around her!

> *"Live out loud" is a phrase I love and I use it often. It is all about what you want more of and what will bring you pleasure. I am a live out loud chick and I want to share with you what that means to me. Somehow there is a sense that "live out loud" literally means being loud but it is actually a declaration of living a life you desire! It is about the shape, texture, and quality of your life. Sometimes it is big life changing events and sometimes it is in the smaller moments that we truly come alive.*
>
> *I am living out loud every time I get behind the wheel of my sexy triple black 6-speed Corvette convertible. I come alive in such a succulent way with the top down and tunes cranked! How I decided to buy this car is also a living out loud story in itself. This was the car my dad was finally going to buy for himself the spring he was killed in a car accident. He had wanted this car for most of his*

Pleasure 101

life and waited for right time to buy it. He and I shared a passion for fast cars. When I received an inheritance check I put it away not wanting it as I was in such a state of grief. One day several years later I saw a commercial for the new corvette...of course it was a triple black. I instantly thought of Dad. I decided in that moment that I would buy that car with the money from Dad. I struggled right up to the moment I wrote out the check. I had never done anything like that just for myself! Certainly there would be many more responsible things to do with the money pay down the mortgage, put in my son's college fund, save it. With some wonderful emotional support from family I went for it. I wasn't g going to wait for the right time, I was going to do it because I wanted it! I have never had a moment of regret. I feel free, wild, powerful, exhilarated and always close to my dad every time I take a cruise. As the song goes, "Life is a highway and I'm gonna drive it!" ~***The Voice of Ann***

At Hot Pink YOUniversity, we seek and wish to share the joy and bliss of living a "pleasure-full" life! We want you to join us in a Hot Pink Pleasure Revolution! It's time for you to create your own **Pleasure Principle!**

> ### Hot Pink Activity 13: Pleasure 101
>
> Google or YouTube the song "Something More" by Sugarland. Turn it up loud and really <u>listen</u> to the lyrics. Enjoy the music, her powerful voice and emotion sink in. If you find it easier you can also google the lyrics after you listen to reference as you write.
>
> Did you have a positive or negative reaction to the lyrics? What do you think this means for you?
>
> What lines hit you the most and why?

How many of our pleasure desires are external or about others, about giving pleasure? And how many of our desired pleasures come from within, about you receiving and are just about your own personal pleasure? If there are not any or few linked to you receiving and coming from within go back and list some!

> "Begin to find and create pleasure in new ways and places. Familiar pleasures are not always the most nourishing choices." ~SARK

At Hot Pink YOUniversity we talk a lot about pushing out of our comfort zones, moving outside the box. Pleasure as we have said, comes in big and small experiences but one thing for sure is that to live out loud and on fire in your pleasure you must include the "new" not just the familiar! What are some kicked up, hot, brand new, never done before pleasures you can go for?

> *"Shortly after filing for divorce after twenty-one years of marriage I flew off to South Beach Miami with my one of my sparkling, juicy, soul sisters and her then eighteen-year-old daughter for a Goddess weekend with Mama*

Gena's School of Womanly Arts. This few amazing days set the tone for feeding my insatiable appetite for sensuality and adventure. I spent my days on the beach soaking in the sun topless and surrounded by the powerful energy of hundreds of women of all shapes, sizes, and walks of life gathered together in a brilliant sisterhood of succulence. Yes, I was topless as in without my bikini top proudly sunning myself and eventually walking right down the beach into the waves with my breasts tanned and bouncing with each step. It was liberating and empowering and oh so much fun to remove my top with my best friend right there joining me. We giggled, wondered, and went for it. I was single for the first time in 23 years. I was in a beautiful place with the unconditional love and energy of my soul sista and all those other women who were in various stages of self-exploration and personal growth. I could feel my power surging and I could honestly say I was loving myself in those moments. I was on fire!"
~The Voice of Ann

Hot Pink Activity 14: Personal Pleasure Principle

Now you are ready to create your very own **Hot Pink Pleasure Principle**. Go back over your journal entries from the last couple days of work on *Want* and *More*. In the first blank below list the two or three things that you want in your life and then look over the entries on ways you can get them, things that bring you pleasure for the second blank. Choose a couple but no worries because you can go back and work on all the things you have listed. We just want to get you started on your Pleasure Revolution!

My Pleasure Principle
I *want more*_____ and I'm gonna get it by _____!

> For a little extra hot inspiration we wanted to share a group **Pleasure Principle** that we created with an amazing gathering of Hot Pink YOUniversity Firestarters at a recent playshop.
>
> "I want more openness, truth, succulence, freedom, power, happiness, joy, spirituality, chance-taking, and adventure seeking. And I'm gonna get it by setting my intentions, seeking those who make me feel safe and trusting, saying no to things that drain my energy, and saying yes to pleasure!"

Create a Hot Pink Pleasure list of things from little and easy to do to the big need to plan for/work toward kind of things. Then commit to doing the little things each day and set a clear plan in place to make sure you get the medium to big planned every so often gift yourself

Bliss! **Create a pleasure list** with the following categories that feed the mind, body and spirit of pleasure. Think of pleasure in small increments and larger time commitments. This will help invite pleasure into your daily life. We shared some of our examples:

Pleasure Quickies (from five minutes to an hour)

- Tapping for emotional freedom (EFT)
- A piece or two or three of chocolate
- Conversation with a friend
- Masturbation
- Aromatherapy (lavender, orange or lemon zest, mint)
- breathing and relaxation

One-Hour Pleasures

- Massage
- Dinner out with yourself

- Painting
- Walk in nature
- Spontaneous sex

One-Day Pleasures

- Field trip to a museum
- Taking pictures
- Swimming
- Hiking
- Skiing
- Antique shopping

Weekend Pleasures

- B & B getaway
- Camping
- Take out a map…pick a trip and be spontaneous
- Home in my jamma's all weekend, get healthy food, awesome movies, wine…

My Dream Big Pleasures

- An Italian getaway
- A week at an art camp
- A photography class
- Making a new best friend
- Learning to play a guitar

Additional Pleasure 101 Rituals and Tools:

- **Start your day** before you get out of bed with a visualization of a pleasure:
- **Create a ritual** of little bliss moments to frame each day. It can be one you want or recalling one you recently experienced.

- **Do a "quick think"!** When you think of the word "Pleasure" what experiences and activities come to mind? Write these down without analyzing or over thinking them. Just put down each thing you can think of. There is a reason you thought of each so honor them! Then use them as a personal guide to building pleasure in your life. Like the Nike commercial says, "*Just Do It!*"
- **Watch for pleasure around you.** Have you seen others or heard others tell stories of pleasure and found yourself wishing for it? What were those and how can you get them in your life? The feelings of envy and jealousy are often indicators of personal longing and desire.
- **Spend a moment or two each day** framing pleasure as a necessary part of your health and well being, not always as a luxury. Retrain your brain to believe in the power of pleasure and it will become routine for you to expect, seek, and receive pleasures from little to big.
- **Do a word association.** Write the word PLEASURE at the top of a page and then think of all the words you can that mean the same or similar…bliss, joy, fun, feel good, etc. Then:
- Make a collage of all the words on a brightly colored (we suggest Hot Pink of course!) poster board and hang it where you can see it often to get your pleasure juices going.
- Write each word on a piece of paper/sticky note and place them where you start your day, end your day and where you spend much time during the day so that you will surround your self with little but powerful "pleasure prompts."
- Collect images, words, phrases, pictures from magazines or printed from online and create your own *Hot Pink Pleasure Board*. This is an instant visualizing tool to help you get in and stay in pleasure.

Women Pleasure Role Models

Think of your own role models throughout history, current, celebrity, family and friends. What do they know, do, exude for pleasure? What have they taught us about adorning our life with all those things that make us feel beautiful and hot? We also want you to recognize the common thread with these women. Their lives were sometimes messy. Their lives had shit sandwiches along the way. These women turned their mess into their message!

"Turn your mess into your message." ~Christie Gause-Bemis

Hot Pink women role models are so important to have. They lead the way, inspire us, invite to think what might be possible and lead by example. We share with you some of our list, but there are many. These are women that create a sense of, "If she can, then I can too."

Amelia Earhart, first female aviator to fly solo across the Atlantic Ocean. This was amazing for the time, the 1930's, when obstacles were plenty. Imagine her critiques and judgments of others, including other women. Amelia reminds us that is in about what others think, but what we desire. She inspired other female aviators to live out their dreams.

Michelle Obama, first lady of the United States. When we think of Michelle the word integrity keeps coming to mind. She kept it real during her husband's term, including her health habits of movement and eating well. She balances her job duties with being a wife and mother. Her message to Hot Pink…keep it real, live with integrity, smile, be healthy and have a sense of humor.

Princess Diana, Princess of Wales. It is through her grace and integrity amidst the pressures of her role that inspires us. Passionate about her causes that she championed. Using her influence to create awareness and change. It is hard enough to leave a marriage without the attention and ridicule of the world watching, imagine the depths of difficulty to strive to have the life she desired; to live authentically as she did in the final years of her life.

Sharon Nalbach, Christie's mother. At a young age, she taught me to be strong, to go after my dreams, to be kind to all and to be a life-long learner. Most importantly, she taught me to live life for me.

Oprah, talk show host and owner of HARPO. She has the ability to elevate those that are in her presence to their greatest BEing. The biggest word that comes to mind: Overcoming. A victim of molestation, growing up in poverty…it is possible. It is possible for all of us to live our dreams.

Marilyn Monroe, actress and icon. You simply see a picture of Marilyn and immediately think of sensuality, sexuality and strength juxtaposed with vulnerability and fragility. Isn't this true for all of us, this yin and yang in all of us. In the 1950s, when women were held to a certain standard of housewife, societal expectations, here unapologetic sexuality pushed the envelope for all of us.

Frida Kahlo de Rivera, Mexican artist known for her self-portraits. Frida exemplifies survivor into thriver. At a young age she was involved in a tragic accident that physically haunted her for the duration of her life. She showed a deep love for her husband, Diego Rivera, also an artist. Her self-portraits showed strength, vulnerability and sensuality. She was also sexually fluid, moving between the feminine and masculine. She inspires us to be creative and romantic.

Pink, singer/songwriter. We love her stage name. Alecia Beth Moore teaches us through her lyrics to be beautiful, that we are perfect, even Fuckin' Perfect. It was through her performance of Glitter in the Air at the Grammies that has been the ultimate inspiration to our Hot Pink Tribe. Bold, brave and talented, she conveys the message to be visible, be authentic, be YOU. Pink also is clearly feminine, yet has masculine qualities to her, to which many women can relate. We don't have to stay within the box created by "others".

Lady Gaga, singer/songwriter. She makes a statement that we can all learn to live by, "I am me-take it or leave it." She does not define herself for other's needs. Her anthem, Born this Way, inspires all of us that we are okay.

Malala Yousafzai, activist for educating women. Shot in Pakistan for being vocal about the need for women to be educated in a country that was run by men and desired to oppress women, she shows extreme bravery. When we tell women to "speak your truth". This is really what we mean. Your voice, your advocacy, what you stand for, who your stand for, is vital life energy. Malala teaches us that to have change, you need to BE the change you seek.

Auril Murgatroyd Harding, Ann's 100 year old grandmother. Matriarch of the family, at 97 she was still chasing around and tubing at the lake with her great grandchildren, at 98 surviving a fire in their family home and making the decision to rebuild, these are amazing feats. It is in how she lived her life as a young woman, leaving home and family to study at a correspondence school and running multiple businesses beginning in the 1950's when very few women did so. She provides Hot Pink a large legacy to live up to. Her motto post fire: "they say you are never too old to start over. Guess we will prove that!" inspires us to believe: If not now, when. If not you, who.

This list is certainly not exhaustive or complete. At our Hot Pink playshops, we often share our full list of women, including their images as we support women to weave their own Sheroes, women who have inspired, taught them to think bigger, dream bigger and women who lead the way. The ability to spark others is something we will dive deeper into in Element IV: Sparking Others. For this moment, we encourage you to seek women who inspire you and take it to the next step to ask yourself why that woman inspires you. We might have friends that are living a life we desire, turn that desire into inspire. We might have friends and family who have overcome, survived, even thrived. Or famous people who have modeled to us something we want for ourselves. What words come to mind and how can you create that in your own Hot Pink life…"I'll have what she's having."

ROSETTA STONE FOR THE HOT PINK TONGUE

Our words are so important for how we frame our life and narrate the present, the past and our future. To create our own narrative, which we will do next, have more pleasure and play in life, how we speak and the words we use to tell our stories can be incredibly powerful. Words have charges of energy connected to them. The choice of words transforms our feeling states.

> *"One time, I was meeting with my good friend Debbie for our writing "group.» (I know. It was just the two of us…and we can generate a lot of good energy with just us two!) We were discussing the power of words as she was talking about all of the things she **had to** do that week which caused her not to write. We talked about changing our "**have to**" to "**get to**" and see if that made a difference for us. When Deb re-narrated with get to, she was able to uncover the things that were filling her up and feeding her the good mojo of life and the things draining her, feeling like an obligation, robbing life of its juiciness. Realizing that she would **get to** have her granddaughter next week, felt alive and good. Realizing she would get to meet deadlines for a certain task felt inauthentic, it was definitely a have to task; one she needed to evaluate and potentially let go in order to tap into the creative spirit and the zest of life." ~The Voice of Christie*

We are going to play around with a couple of our favorite and most powerful reframes:

Changing "have to" to "get to"

The difference will provide clarity on those things that are truly drains on us and need to be reevaluated or let go. Sometimes, just reframing our "have to" to "get to", turns it into something alive and enjoyable.

Changing *"I'm sorry but"* to *"I'm sorry and. ..."*

When you add a "but" to anything, it negates what came before that. "I love your new scarf, but...,» "I know we are friends, but...." You get the picture. Take the "but's" out of your life. You will be showing unconditional positive regard for others and yourself.

Changing "if I graduate" or "if I travel to Ireland" to "when I graduate," or "when I travel to Ireland."

When you have a dream and a desire, say **when. When** puts forward all of your energy and positive attention and intention into the direction of your desire.

Changing drama words to moderate words

Did you ever talk to someone and hear them narrate their story using words like: "Oh, it was just awful." "I was horrified." "It was traumatizing!"? And then you discover that she was talking about not finding a parking space, or being late for a meeting, or not coming home to a clean house. Let's put these daily things into perspective and give them the words they deserve: inconvenient, embarrassing, and upsetting. When we moderate our words, we moderate our emotions, perceive things in the way they are meant to be perceived. We will save the big words in life for the truly big things.

Change can't to won't.

Can't is a choice. Any time you use the word "can't." you are making a choice. Sometimes this can be in a positive way, for example, when you are setting a boundary for yourself, saying "no" to something that does not resonate with your intentions for the self. It is important to be clear that this is a personal choice, a bold choice, an intentional choice, "No, I can't do ____." And that is okay…own it! Sometimes "can't" rears its head from a negative place out of fears or selfimposed limitations, "I can't take that trip to _____." So not true! If your goal/dream/intention is important enough, you **will** find a way. **Can't** is always a choice!

Changing try to will

When we try to do something we are not putting our full energies into it. When we **will** something there are defined goals, micro-steps, and deadlines around that goal.

In fact, while we are at let's make up some new words for just us. Here are a few and feel free to come up with a few more, we would love for you to share with our Facebook community, any powerful reframes you have discovered or created.

Change deadlines to lifelines

"When I meet that lifeline for my new book, it will feel uplifting!" Our Firestarter, Lisa Krupp, shared her reframe of deadline to climax, which really does make it a little juicier to meet.

Change Bucket List to Life List

You are not dead yet! It is a reframe on the expansion of time versus creating a scarcity of time that we are all lead to buy into. A life list, keeps it among the living. A life list keeps you into BEing and DOing, not just something fun for someday, but or NOW.

Friends to Soul Sisters

Soul sisters deepens the connection hat we have with true friendships. It honors the connection in a way that "best friends" does not. We can have many soul sisters in our lives, not one being the best, each offering different things for different needs. In Element IV: Sparking Others, we will share our secrets for how to create more of these connections.

Juicy to Juicified

If we are juicified, we are lit up, turned on, our juices are flowing and life feels amplified. Greater joy. Abundance pleasure.

Become more aware of the words that you use. Catch yourself with word choices and do an immediate reframe. Feel what follows internally and emotionally when you use the reframe. Be aware of words that hold charges for you, trigger you, positively or negatively. What story is behind that word. When we were first working with one of our Firestarters, she had a serious aversion to the word juicy. Further explored, that trigger comes from the story of sexuality and whether it okay to express. Words that make us think, "that's naughty", are usually derived from our past experience, our beliefs that may no longer be valid and might even hold us back.

THE POWER OF OUR NARRATIVES

During a recent Hot Pink Burn Baby Burn Playshop, we sat around the campfire and told stories. In order to illustrate the power of our stories, we will share with you the following experience as shared by Christie that night:

> *"In 1996, two very significant things happened to me: I lost my sister to cancer and I made the decision I needed to leave my husband. He was awful to me in many ways and I can't believe I married him. "Why does this always happen to me?" went through my head often. I felt abandoned and lost. The only good thing that came out of that marriage was my son. The divorce was hard and I lost so much, my home, a lot of my stuff and time with my son. The world is so hard. Sometimes I don't even know why I keep trying. It never turns out well. If I could go back, I would never have married him in the first place."*
> *~as shared that night by Christie*

Hot Pink Activity 15A: Old Stories

Take five minutes to write your story. A life changer, an event or situation that caused you pain. Write that now. *"Once upon a time...."*

The story above is filled with all those recurrent themes: victim, loss, abandonment, a world of hardship. Often as women, we gather and that is how we share our stories. "This happened **to** me." We lose our power, we hand off our control, we are the victim of our circumstances. It is all very disempowering. And, to expect life to not have moments of vulnerabilities, loss and struggle is kind of crazy if you think about it. That's life. If there is one guarantee we will give you… *You* will have pain, *You* will have hurt, *You* will have loss. There is no getting around that, avoiding it. In fact, it is a sign that you have been living a plugged in life, that you have loved well, that you have lived full on and out loud! *You* have lived Hot Pink! To feel *all* those human emotions, the good, the bad, the ugly! Great *job* darling!

So, now it is time to narrate our lives from a place of strength, power and courage. Here is the reframe from the story we shared.

> *"In 1996, two amazing life changes occurred for me. My beautiful, older sister Michelle, ended her two year battle with brain cancer surrounded by her family and our love. It is incredible to bear witness to the birth of a new soul and just as incredible to be with a personwhen they make that transition from this life to the next. I am so grateful I was a part of that. I wish there were easier, less painful ways to learn life's lessons, but there is not and I honor that time in my life. It allowed me to reevaluate what I wanted the next stage in my life to look like. I realized, through that experience, I was strong, I was fierce, I was vulnerable, I deserved happiness and I deserved to beloved. I left a marriage that no longer served me, grew me, loved me. It was hard because in leaving I knew I may have to give up everything to then later have everything. I honor the man I was married to for being in my life as a fellow soul, so that I could learn what I needed to from that relationship. No regrets, it is all a journey. When I look at my gorgeous son now, I feel total satisfaction. When I look at the reflection in the mirror, I honor the choices I have made as being the best choice I could possibly make, given what I knew at that time and the lesson I needed was given to me, through a relationship,*

a situation, an event, through a choice." ~ as retold by Christie

Now that is a kickass way to look at your life. How did the narration make you feel? YOU can do this too! It is a choice you must make as a beautiful, luscious, Hot Pink woman! How do you want to narrate your life?

Hot Pink Activity 15B: Your New *Hot Pink* Story

Look again at the event you first wrote about. What lessons did you learn from it? What came out of it or continues to come out of it? How did it make you strong or fierce? Or could if you let it? This may take some time, some courage and even, maybe, some forgiveness. But that forgiveness is a gift you give to yourself to set you free! Your anger and hurt at others is doing nothing to them and everything to you. *You* are not a victim here, *You* are a goddess of immeasurable strength.

Now rewrite that story Hot Pink Style!

"Once upon a time...

There is always something to learn, new ways to grow. There is always a message or a lesson in what happens in life. When we live with that belief, there is a surrender to the chaos, need to control, need to know. BE A HOT PINK GODDESS!

TRANSFORMATION THROUGH TRAVEL

Travel is Hot and Juicy when you choose trips that take you out of your comfort zone, when you travel with the intention of transformation, and when you allow for the three phases of travel to unfold for you.

There are always three phases of travel that give rise to each trip we take. There is the planning, the actual trip itself and the memories created as the aftermath of our travels. The planning is the anticipation, the building adrenaline as the day comes closer, the pouring over the travel books and imagining the sights to be seen, the food to eat, the experiences. This planning phase can be a favorite part of the trip. You just get a rush as dreaming of what you may experience. The faces of those whom you tell, "Yeah, I'm going to Costa Rica, next week," and the look of envy as you prepare for your departure. These are all the "hot and juicy" moments created by living your dream and manifesting travel. The aftermath of travel, the memories, the photos, the look of envy on people's faces when you say, "Yeah, I just got back from London." But, the moment of the actual trip elevates our spirit to just be in the moment. To experience the what is, not the what **was** or what **will** be…to just *Be*.

> "Travel is the one thing you can buy that makes you richer."
> ~Anonymous

> *"As I departed on my latest adventure to Italy and Greece with the Travel with Jana group, I just wanted to be in the moment. The two days prior to joining the group, I spent with my ever-positive and positively fun soul sister,*

> *Diane. The adventure of driving a manual car through the Sorrento and Amalfi Coast, these two days made me feel free, strong, and in awe at the beauty of the world. We spent 40 minutes one rainy night, parking this car in the smallest of spaces on the planet. There were moments of utter frustration and triumph in our persistence. We drove the narrowest of roads, saw amazing vistas, and enjoyed a two and a half hour lunch just BEing."*
> *~The Voice of Christie*

If you travel in a group, you learn to rely on one another and these are some of the lessons you can take away from traveling:

There are people in this world who are hopeful, positive and ecstatic to be alive. People who love to travel shift into such a positive vibration on our Hot Pink travel trips.

> *"You are the average of the five people you spend the most time with."*
> *~Jim Rohn*

During travel, and especially with Hot Pink YOUniversity, your average goes sky high. Trips like the ones we have taken, attract people who love their lives and use words like: manifest and law of attraction and live your dreams. We kind of like that we live in a world with people who take 100% responsibility for their current state of mind and the direction of their future. Who are not afraid of a little fear as being a sign of growth. Who use the valleys of their lives to be even greater than who they were before the "thing" happened for them.

Christie and Ann in Turkey, 2014.

In this wide, wide world, travel actually decreases the perception of size, disconnect, and differences of the world and it becomes expansive and small all at the same time. We are all simply beings connected by such common threads. And, the more we travel, the more we realize how simple life and the world really is. We all want love, we all want joy, we all want some companionship. The only thing different is the form these all take. When each of us first started traveling we envisioned all the exotic things we would take in and the different lifestyles we would encounter. From playing with school children in Vietnam to orphans in Bali to sitting on a patio restaurant in Italy and talking to the owner about how his mother fled to the hills in World War II, to dancing the chicken dance and shooting hoops with Turkish children in the middle of a school day, the common theme of connection and telling our stories is woven through the various textures of our travels.

There is so much to see and we want to see it all. Is it possible to see every nook and cranny of this beautiful world? If it were so, we want to see. It feeds us, it fills us and makes us feel fully alive. If you could all find something in life that fills you with passion, isn't that what is important? Travel is the one thing that can never make you feel bored. Whether that passion is travel, cooking, eating, creating, learning, raising your children, reading, connecting, finding your "**It**" is the important thing. Feeling "**It**" and living "**It**." Not waiting for someday when the stars all line up—but, now.

Support of your loved ones is nice…but what if *everyone* is not on board. Not everyone is going to be on board with your passions 100% of the time. Does that mean you put them to the side and acquiesce? or, do you move forward and try your best to compassionately understand and yet not compromise your perspective and desires. A woman on one of our trips, Kim Moriyama, shared this concept that sums up how we choose to show up in our relationships: "It is my intention to keep my focus on you, while still honoring my truth and co-create in this space together." Isn't that a beautiful thing? It is about intention. It is not an intention to hurt anyone, husband, kids, friends, or anyone else in your life, with the decisions you may make. Travel may be one, and so many of the women we work with, desire to see the world and to travel. Yet, they hold back and wait for the "right" time. Even if others in your life are not on board for whatever the reason, if travel fills your soul, your loved ones will find a way to come on board, or not. And you can still love them, and they can still love you. You can support those you love the best you can, the rest is up to them. Kim credits this knowledge she shared with a workshop she attended on Abraham Hick's Law of Attraction. This is one of the many examples of beautiful people and messages you meet along the way.

The last stage of travel happens once you are back at home and the memories that were made, lessons along the way. In this stage it is important to honor our trips and to successfully transition back to our home, our loved ones and our routines, but in new ways. We need to integrate our knowledge that was gained in meaningful and intentional ways. By doing this, our travel experiences live on. Putting picture on the walls you see everyday keeps you tapped into the experience. Gathering together your travel companions after you return home integrates the experiences. Bringing home a bottle of wine and opening it during a meal a month later, revives the memories made. This third stage is just as important as the overall experience of travel.

Our Hot Pink India Trip Tribe, Sunrise on the Ganges, 2015

We want to share with you just a few of our favorite traveling experiences with Hot Pink YOUniversity, by ourselves and in other groups:

- Experiencing the tantric temples of Khajuraho, India.
- Together, standing naked and proud in a group of amazing women telling my body beautiful story at a Pamela Madsen, Back to the Body Retreat in New Orleans. ~Ann
- Morning sunrise and music on the Ganges in India.

- Hiking 10 miles through the rice fields of Bali to swim in a waterfall. Then return back to our village housing and have a skinny dipping pool party with the other women in our group. ~Christie
- Staying in a hostel overlooking the San Francisco bridge, a $200 view for $11 for the night. ~Christie
- Touring the island of Cozumel with our Hot Pink Tribe, snorkeling as meditation playshop, and visiting the ruins of San Gervasio and Goddess Ixchel.

Travel does not need to be an expensive endeavor. There are many creative ways to manifest the money towards travel and to travel in a way that is affordable.

Here are some Hot Pink Travel ideas:

Group travel can be more affordable in many ways as you can get group discounts and share rides, as well as other costs. Order a meal with 5 others and try a little of everything. Share a hotel room. Share a shuttle to the airport. Share a guide for the day.

Choose your country. There are so many affordable countries in which to travel. Do some research and find what is affordable right now. Thailand, Vietnam, India…are just of few.

Shoulder seasons. The high season is winding down and deals can be had.

Hostel, Airbnb. We shared a hostel room in India for about $16 a night including our breakfasts. And, our roommate, an Italian man wearing only a towel when we first met him… OoooLaLa.

These ideas are not for everyone. There are ways to manifest the money that is needed for travel. If you have a skill or a service or a product, we believe that you are two months away from being okay or from manifesting some extra money for these experiences.

HONORING YOUR BODY BEAUTIFUL

"There is no such thing as an ugly woman."
~Vincent Van Gogh

So let's talk about this Body Beautiful! We know, not the easiest of topics! We are not going to linger long at the mirror asking you to dig deep and explore what you don't like or what your obstacles are to loving your body and then journal on it because truly we all know we have done that over and over for years! We are going to challenge you, Hot Pink style, to change your thinking and try new ways to care for your body and love the skin you're in! We made a promise to ourselves, and our Firestarter sisters, that when we look in the mirror we are *really* gonna look! Not at the parts that in the past we would cringe, hide, fear, obsess over; but, *all* our parts in a fresh, juicy, wonderful new way. *Getting juicy with our wonderful selves*

"Curve the loveliest distance between two points."
~Mae West

We are committed to loving our bodies these days—at all the glorious sizes and incarnations they take at any given time. After all, we are women we are on a brilliantly ever evolving journey through life and so are our bodies. They are our living breathing map, our sculpture of all our life stories. Our bodies hold such amazing wisdom, knowledge and lessons of all we have felt, experienced and created along the way and it shows! They are brilliant in their variation. We can learn from our bodies at every age, stage, size and state of health we find ourselves in.

Think about seeing your body that way next time you look in the mirror. What stories does it tell? What lessons can you learn? This is so much better for us than analyzing our parts under a false set of criteria driven not by nature and health; but, by the marketing machine of pop culture and the media. We need to embrace our whole self all the great stuff and the tough stuff too. As women, we are bombarded over and over with images of what the "perfect" female body should be. Those images are so far from the real bodies of real woman that we all tend to become pretty distorted in our body image. We pressure ourselves into this narrow image portrayed in the media of what the "perfect" female body is. Not only are we raised to be self conscious of our "size" but also of our actual parts!

> **"My actual parts are perfect in each imperfection."**
> **~Hot Pink Body Mantra**

We all have a "true weight and shape," the one that our bodies want to be at naturally when we are taking really good care of ourselves. This is uniquely our own and is beautifully different than others. This is the true Body Beautiful! It is firm, soft, round, old, lined, long, short, tall, young, smooth, curvy, lithe, lean, light, solid, small…the list goes on. We all know there is this individual uniqueness, this predestined shape that is called forth from our genetics, our ancestors, our ethnicity. I say embrace this shape. *Your* shape. *Your* Body Beautiful.

> **Hot Pink Activity 16: Embrace Your Shape**
>
> Apple   Pear   Hourglass   Straight
>
> A-cup, B-cup, No-cup, C-cup, D-cup
>
> Lanky   Vavavoom   Like my motha'   Bu-donka-donk-donk
>
> Bodacious   Delicious   Buddhalicious   Junk in da' trunk
>
> Whootwooooo   Round   Inverted triangle   Short   Tall   Curvy
>
> Hummana Hummana Ahhhhh!

So, we will walk the walk and talk the talk. Here, in our own voices we will tell just bit of our Hot Pink body beautiful stories to encourage you to do the same. You will see how gloriously diverse we are and yet how very much the same in our journeys to body beautiful. This is a powerful example of the very core of our Hot Pink message. We are all who we are, what we look like, and what we believe in yet a growing sisterhood—a tribe of women coming into our power and learning to dig the skin we are in! Go ahead, read our stories and then start writing your own. Look at your body and listen to it. What does it tell you? What memories does it call forth? What is it teaching you? What is it desiring? Write your story!

> *"I am 5 foot, 2 inches. I have a bodacious bod. I am a goddess. I honor my 36-double Ds, my 36-inch hips and my waist that at times could be contributing to that hourglass figure and at times fill in a bit and offer my lover a place to dwell. I have a round tummy and just below my belly button are silvery little stretch marks that I now embrace as badges of courage and honor for growing and birthing a great big healthy baby boy who is now a*

handsome 6 foot man! I smile and allow myself to get lost in the story of my son when I look at my tummy! I have a voluptuous chest which is pretty noticeable on a short girl. I am blessed to still sport just that bit of a tear drop droop. I got those from my Mom. My breasts are now like hers. When I look at my chest sometimes I find myself remembering my Momma with a smile. I have curves. Whether I am harder and firmer or softer and fuller, I am always Mae West packed into a little frame and I rock it!
~The Voice of Ann

I grew up super skinny...twigs for arms, twigs for legs... teased for my hairy arms, dubbed by my sister as "gorilla arms". I shaved them in third grade...a story often recounted by my family publicly and humiliatingly. I wanted to look like Valerie Bertinelli or Farah Fawcett, or anyone else but me. I never developed, never got boobs, and was then dubbed a new nickname. "Double A" in high school by pubescent brutal boys whom I wished thought I was sexy and beautiful and wantable. It was not until the last decade that I have embraced who I am and how I was made.

Despite all the times my mother said I was beautiful— and I did believe it—I also believed what my peers fed me and the media pushed it like a dealer on the corner.

Fast forward to a January 3, 2006 journal entry:

    Ok, here's the deal: my ass is thirty-five years old. It is similar to my mother's at that age. And, I have been trying, unsuccessfully to fit it into my jeans I wore at age 25. Today, I have set my ass free a revolution of sorts! I have made a decision to shop for clothes in the "age appropriate" section of the store. Juniors?! No more! I have received a compliment on my lady jeans already. My crotch can breathe. "Ahhhhhh" it is saying.

> *I now embrace my body and strive for healthy—for me, for my age, for what feels vibrant and loving to me. I have occasional twinges of comparisons and wish my curves were a little less curvaceous. We pluck, we nip, we tuck and pull all to become anything but that which we are. It is time to embrace our package that houses our internal spirit!*
> *~The Voice of Christie*

We want to share with you a couple tools to help you build a loving, succulent relationship with your body in all it's amazing, miraculous and beautiful forms and incarnations. It is every woman's right to love her glorious deliciousness. It is every woman's destiny to dance though life! If we are to grow, radiate and flourish, we need to love the skin we are in!

Activities to Increase Your Body Beautiful

Stand in front of a full length mirror naked. Simply observe. No judgment. Look. Turn sideways, turn around, confront your full frontal nudity. What do you love about this temple of yours? Start at the eyes. Look at their depth, shape, color and the story they tell. Move down to your mouth. Thin lips, full lips, one bigger than the other? These lips frame your smile. Smile wide and bright. Your teeth. Crooked, straight, artificially straightened, white, yellowed, somewhere in between? Look at your teeth and lips. They give you such character and can say so much about what you are feeling and thinking at any given time. They are your source for biting into life! Move down to your shoulders. Hunched, straight backed, squared, rounded. The shoulders carry the weight of our world. They are strong and solid. Move to your chest. Gaze at your breasts. Tits, taataa's, titties, lady pillows, headlights, jugs, fun bags, boobs, cans…the list goes on. One bigger than the other? Only one or maybe none there to see? Brown nipples, pink nipples or your very own unique shade? These breasts, two, one or this chest, is yours. None are alike…literally! Enjoy the roundness, longness, softness, firmness, the mounds or the flat, the stretch marks, the dimples, the scars…these too are yours alone and tell your story. Move to your core. Smile as you enjoy your belly. The solar plexus. The third chakra. Is it round, firm, soft, flabby, rippled, smooth, dimpled? This belly of yours is your center. It is perfect for you and home to the organs that keep you functioning day in and day out. Take in your hips. The succulent soft way they curve in the very essence of the female form. The cradle to hold babies, the curve where your lovers hand grabs and dwells. Love these woman curves. Now head south of the border. The vagina. The vajayjay. The groin, pussy, beaver, snatch, yoni, poonani, twat, lady hump, the MmmmHmmm. Again, the list goes on as does the power of this amazing part of our female form. Go ahead and grab a hand mirror and place it on the floor. Squat over the mirror. We know, we know…something we just don't do. This is foreign territory for many of us. The only person who should be looking at that thing is the OB/GYN or your lover, right? Nope! It's for you and of you. This pussy of yours is the epicenter of the Universe the Yoniverse, the YOUniverse! Where life begins. Lovers long to be inside this sacred garden, babies emerge from this sacred garden. Don't be afraid of it. Enjoy the colors, shape, and unique beauty of your vagina. Move on to the legs, knees and feet. Strong, weak, slim, large, they carry your forward and ground you to this earth. These appendages walk you through life and are deserving of your utmost respect.

 We encourage you to do this exercise, take this visual and deeply moving journey over your body each day for twenty-one days. Over that time you will begin to really get to know yourself in a way that is foreign to most women. It is an intimate bonding of mind body spirit that will lead you on the path of loving this body of yours. This temple. This sanctuary of your soul. This map of your life stories. This—*Your* Body Beautiful!!

A cast rendering of our Body Beautifuls, Camp WOW, 2013

Check out Tara Lynnone of the first highly successful in the mainstream and most outspoken models to embrace her true shape in an industry dominated by extremes in body weight and image. She emanates the Body Beautiful message and we love her for it!

Music

Just a few deeply moving songs that we feel embody a strong Body Beautiful message…Are there other songs you can think of that truly celebrate the female body? We encourage you to do a YouTube search to get the video clips with streaming lyrics as you listen!

"Beautiful" by Christina Aguilera
"Fuckin' Perfect" by Pink
"Healed, Whole and Healthy" by Karen Drucker
"Your Body is a Wonderland" by John Mayer (beautiful love song…but try the lyrics in first person…sing them using I, me, my! A love song to ourselves and our body!)

What did these lyrics bring up for you? Thoughts and feelings…

Artistic Activity

Find a piece of artwork of the female form/body that speaks deeply to you and buy it for your home. Display it in a prominent location to encourage empowerment and self love. By the way….everyone loves the beauty of the female body in art!

Have a professional photographer take artistic photos of you or an artist to paint, sketch or draw you to highlight your Body Beautiful—naked, adorned, clothed in deeply sensual, sexy, pretty lingerie or clothes. Whatever will push you to honor your truly beautiful form. Gift this to yourself—and your lover will get the gift as well! Hang this intimate and wonderful piece in a special space in your home such as your bedroom, studio or master bath.

There, we have laid ourselves bare for you…we are naked and sharing how we now want to adorn ourselves. We have examined all the darknesses, the shit sandwiches, the junk that has limited our ability to love our bodies and hey, if you aren't loving your body then on a core level you aren't loving yourself. The journey to Body Beautiful is such an important part of Hot Pink journey. Here's to loving the skin your in!!

> *"I will say, I am fired up on an entirely new and deeper level since returning from my adventure in New Orleans at the Back to the Body Sensual Retreat for Women (BttB) lead by Pamela Madsen and her amazing team! I have spent a lot of time teaching and sharing about Hot Pink Body Beautiful and sacred sensuality in the past and feel good about what I have shared. I am feeling even more in touch with, in tune to and in love with my body. It is showing up in little, middle and big ways. I am a changed woman! I wanna share this juicy good stuff with every woman I can! I cannot speak enough to the power of this activity. I know from personal experience!! I recently blogged about the power of being photographed. Here is my story: I gifted myself a truly "Hollywood" experience while in New Orleans. I*

purchased an hour of full professional hair and makeup and an hour with an internationally known powerhouse photographer to capture me, my body, my personal energy and sensuality in a photoshoot. I was nervous and way out of my comfort zone! He took several hundred shots. I felt like a super model, sex goddess, queen and I ROCKED it!! I moved my body to the sounds of Prince blasting through the sexy master bedroom and bathroom of the luxurious historic home we stayed in for the 6 blissful days of the BttB retreat. I opened myself to the sensual directions of the photographer as he said things like, "I want you to imagine your lover walking in to see you like this, waiting for him, framed in the sunlight." "Turn and arch a bit more so the sunlight captures the sexy curve of your breast." I can feel a stirring in me as I write this! A girl doesn't forget these moments! My body and I were center stage and I was truly a Hot Pink Sensual Goddess capturing my core essence and presenting my body in a moment of sheer joy. I am so excited to create pieces of art for our home, to share some of these images proudly with our Hot Pink Tribe and to create a special photo book for my lover. (Shhhhh...it's a surprise!) I will say that I genuinely believe every woman should do this at least once...preferably more than once in her life!" ~*The Voice of Ann*

Element III: Burn, Baby, Burn!

OOOOOooooooo…We can feel it! A fire is coming alive inside YOU!

This is our personal favorite Element of all! This is it ladies where all that fire building up in volcanic combustion is sizzling and ooozzzing and bursting forward. NO APOLOGIES! Hear me roar! Check out one of our favorite turns us on songs "Roar" by Katy Perry

Crank it loud. Get up—and dance!!!!

There are always going to be people, places, jobs, events and stuff holding you down. But, you don't have to be held down. That is no longer your first choice or modus operandi. Got it!? It is time to really live out loud and this Element is all about it. YOU are unstoppable. Enjoy it!

MANIFESTING BIG DREAMS & ATTRACTING YOUR DESIRES

"Those who dream by day are cognizant of many things which escape those who dream only by night…"
~Edgar Allen Poe

Have you ever just watched a young girl play dress up? Twirling in a blur of soft pink organza as a plastic tiara is perched precariously upon her soft curls. In that moment she is not only playing princess, she IS the princess. Or how about a young boy in his cape and mask, a super hero sent to save the world. In that moment, he is not just a little boy in a costume. He IS the superhero who will save the world. At Hot Pink YOUniversity we are all good with boys in tutus and tiaras and girls in capes and masks too! It's all about whatever gets your juices flowing!

Dreaming big was an important part of each of our childhoods. It's what got us through the early years. Remember hearing, "What do you want to be when you grow up?» And our response was as vast as the night sky. We had no filter. We were not tainted. We dreamt of all the wonderful options. Time and space ceased to exist when we were given the opportunity to share our dreams. We could truly become anything or anybody we desired. The world was ours. There was no question of time, money, education, socioeconomic status or gender. Yet along the path of life time, age, society, teachers, bullies, and even perhaps, our well-meaning parents have left us jaded. Jaded by the false belief that dreams were just that—dreams. A dream was something that happened at night in your sleep and it wasn't real.

At Hot Pink YOUniversity, we see things a little differently. We know it is your dreams and your visions that fuel you to move forward. If it weren't for your dreams you would be stuck in a life that was not bringing you joy, not feeling authentic. You would be making others happy, but not yourself. Dreams are the foundation upon which all life is experienced. Dreams are the reflection of our soul's deepest longings. To dim, dumb or doubt down our dreams is like placing a cinch around our soul. It depletes the life force within us. Dreams are the framework of a life well lived. A life on fire. A Hot Pink life!

> *"Don't let anyone or anything Dim, Dumb or Doubt you down!"*
> *~Ann Murgatroyd Soe*

But alas, dreaming and dreaming *Big*, require courage. Dreams require you to get out of your comfort zone. Dreams ask you to explore and examine yourself. Dreams require you to trust. Dreams require you to forgive. Dreams require you to let go of things, people, jobs that no longer serve you. Dreams require us to embrace and accept what cannot be changed in order to focus on what can. Dreams demand your attention. Dreams are fragile and require constant care. Dreams beckon you to play and connect with the child within. Dreams are almost like a dare. Dreams call you to take a risk!

When your dreams are derailed or veer off course, you can get discouraged. You might lose that trust in the Universe and the YOUniverse. Or question the law of attraction. You never stop to consider that maybe, just maybe, that dream you held wasn't meant for your highest good? You then begin to question just who do I really think I am to have such notions? How did my pysche get so wounded, so fragile? And when did I begin to believe that building a stone wall around my wounded and fragile psyche was the way to live a full life? Do you not teach our children to get back up after they fall? Do you not encourage our youth to try and try again? Do you not kiss your young adult child on her way to college and whisper to her that she can be anything her heart desires? If so, why is it so hard for us as women to practice what we preach?

Dreaming takes courage. You must birth yourself out of the cocoon of fear that has entrapped you for way too long. As you birth yourself into the art and science of dreaming you step outside your comfort zone, it then becomes necessary to take the cocoon shell and set it ablaze. In Element I, you were required to release limiting beliefs, to create new limitless beliefs. In Element II, you focused on increasing your pleasure, prosperity and tap into what you deserve. Now we are moving into looking at your dreams and high expectations for your life. Fear, is truly the bad "F-word" (And if you haven't guessed, we like the other F-word!). It paralyzes a person emotionally and spiritually. When you begin to live a life on fire, you may hear a bold voice in our heart asking, "*Who are you **not** to dream, beautiful one?!*"

> "*The Future Belongs to Those Who Believe in the Beauty of Their Dreams.*"
> ~*Eleanor Roosevelt*

It is our guess that you are reading this and joining us in this Hot Pink adventure to break free. To grow. To let go of the past and all that holds you back so you may spring forth a new and improved version of you with a fresh, vibrant energy and a deeper sense of courage, determination and self-confidence. Well, there's good news and bad news. The good news is, all this is possible and then some! The bad news, it's gonna take some work. We simply cannot lie. Learning to not only dream but nurture those dreams and holding tight to a deep conviction of them is not only the starting point, it is the journey and the destination. This isn't a process one simply masters and then life just rolls along in a whole new glorious direction. While one CAN master the process, it will forever require your attention, devotion and discipline. It will require you, over and over again to step outside your comfort zone, your known zone and into what our soul sister, Jana Stanfield calls the "Ohhhhh Zone." This is where all the best, juiciest stuff happens for us!

So here's the scoop sister—Dream and **Dream Big**! You have earned and deserve to live out your dreams. It's the portal to manifesting the kicked up, full throttle life on fire that we all desire. But if those dreams seem too distant, too unattainable, then it's time to take a look at your comfort zone. The relationship we have with our zone of comfort is what keeps us from becoming the Creatrix of our life, or it can become what throws us into the center of our own flame and our YOUniverse so that we burn brighter as we live one helluva hot life!

Hot Pink Activity 17: Dream Big!

If fear were not a factor, I would…
If I were brave, I would…

List 100, Yes, you heard us right—100 things I would do, visit, experience, try, create, feel, be…Fill up this page!
Dream Big, Bountiful Dreams   Gorgeous!

Original artwork by Christie Gause-Bemis

*"You are confined by the boundaries that you set yourself.
The mind creates the cage.
Set yourself free and move out of your comfort zone…"
~Mhar*

Recently, a Firestarter shared her story of dreaming with us that illustrates the need to release and let go of expectations for self and others and allow dreams to get big and bold.

"I have a job. A career even, and it's a good one. I help people, am well respected, have a lot of responsibility, and am generously compensated. I spent almost a decade studying, stressing, and working hard to attain the career in which I've been employed for the last 24 years. After some reflection, it's as if my life were this beautifully orchestrated sequence of events that effortlessly guided me down a path of conventional wisdom. Follow the rules, play it safe, do what's expected, perform well, and you will (hopefully) be rewarded with a job you will be "privileged to enjoy" for a minimum of 40 hours per week for rest of your able-bodied adult life. Ideally, that job allows you to pay your bills, live with a sense

of comfort and security, and afford a few extra luxuries along the way.

The oft unspoken dogma of health care is that if you're not working your mind and body to the bone, you're not doing it right. There is pride in the martyrdom and unrealistic expectations of sleeplessness, overwork, life imbalance, and dangerous multi-tasking. This paradigm sucked the life out of me and I felt ashamed that I wasn't like everyone else and that I wanted something more. I wanted less stress, less work, and less demands. I wanted more flexibility, more sleep, more predictability, more autonomy, more passion, more soulfulness, and more authenticity. I wanted work that fed my soul, not drained it. I wanted to feel lit up by my work, not beaten down by it. I had no idea what direction I needed to take to change my circumstances, but I knew I needed to do something, so I offered up a plea for guidance to the universe and waited.

I believe to the depths of my being that we can't move into something new for ourselves until we step out of the old that is holding us back. We must create space (emotionally, spiritually, and physically) for new opportunities to present themselves. Faith matters. In yourself and in the power that rules the universe. Manifestation of your desires is real, but it needs faith, patience, and courage as its fuel. We have all of that within us and it's up to us to unlock it.

Instead of "how dare you want more?"…how dare you NOT live your truth or create your life, no matter what conventional wisdom and the world has to say."
~The Voice of Alyssa Tesar

If you want something you have never had, then you must be willing to do something you have never done.
~Thomas Jefferson

In order for those dreams that are drifting around inside your head to come to fruition, you may be required to step out of your comfort zone. To walk on the wild side. To feel uncomfortable—temporary discomfort only, please. We are all about pleasure around here!. To trust. The comfort zone is the cage. Your dreams are the song bird trapped inside. It's time to open the cage door and take flight!

The comfort zone is one selfish little bitch! She simply wants to own us forever. To keep you small, to keep you down and to avoid any amount of discomfort. If you avoid discomfort at all costs, it will eventually cost you a great deal, your hopes, your dreams, your purpose and your potential.

Another woman we have worked with in our Woman on Fire Program, Laurie, dreams to have greater freedom than what her current structured job provides. She had a year of momentary discomfort, working full-time and going back to school for massage. She is hoping to combine her love of massage with a women's wellness, opening a home studio and cutting back or leaving her full-time job all together. Something she had never thought possible when living with old beliefs about responsibility and society's boxes.

GETTING OUT OF YOUR COMFORT ZONES AND JUMPING INTO YOUR FLAME

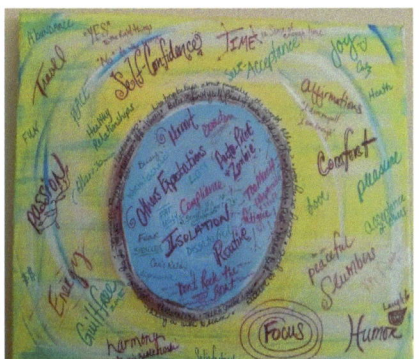

This is an art piece we made at a recent Soup and Soulfood, a gathering of our Hot Pink Women…. In the center are where we are now…*living in others expectations, compliance, don't rock the boat, auto-pilot*. Outside the circle is where we want to be, to grow, to dream to…*comfort, pleasure, passion, travel, yes, abundance*. Around the circle are comfort zones, edges I have chosen not to cross: *Routines, worries, fears, money, swimming naked, laughing at my own jokes, talking to a stranger, being alone, failing, trying something new, traveling to another country, spending money on me, saying no, being hurt, vulnerable or scared, rollercoasters, letting go of stuff or others, leaving.*

This is where your gorgeous dreams go....

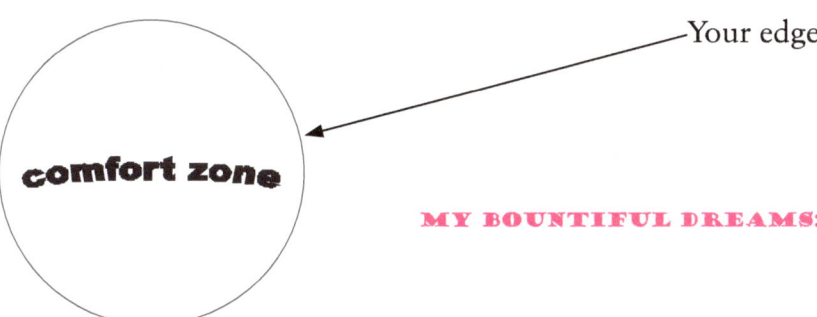

Your edge

MY BOUNTIFUL DREAMS:

Hot Pink Activity 18: Comfort Zones

Listen to: Jana Stanfield's songs "If I Were Brave" and "What Would I Do If I Had No Fear."

Sometimes if you lose track of your dreams, or your comfort zone gets in the way of you reaching for those dreams, another sister's support, encouragement and love can put it all back into perspective. That's why we build sisterhoods among other women who are our biggest cheerleaders. It is the **Hot Pink Vibe of the Tribe.** There are more than enough people on the planet willing to steal your dreams, or dim dumb, or doubt you down. There are plenty of reasons why you could stay all wrapped up in your comfort zone and live from fear. A Hot Pink sister will never tell you to not reach for the stars. What she will tell you is "That's a big hell yes!" "Go for it!" Make sure you surround yourself with Hot Pink Women.

There are some effective ways to keep yourself on track with actualizing your dreams and stepping out of your comfort zone:

CLARITY. Get clear on what you want. What are you really craving? What are you really longing for? What will leave you with that feeling, "Okay, I can die happy now." Define your dreams. They may seem small or they may seem insurmountable. Do not judge. Again, do not judge. Wash, rinse, repeat. You get the picture. Write them down, record them. Create a life list with your to urgent desires and as well as another life list with your future dreams. Cross them off the list as they begin to manifest. Add to the list, delete from the list, adjust the list. There are no rules. This is your life, and you call the shots. Dreams, passions and desires change. Take stock of this quarterly for yourself. In *The PassionTest*, by Janet and Chris Atwood, they take you through a step by step process on getting clear with what you desire. If done quarterly, you can live your life full of intentional action versus aimlessly and on autopilot. Get out of being a passenger in your life and take active steps and intentional thoughts and movements towards that which you desire. It is all up to you!

KEEP YOUR EYES ON THE PRIZE. Keeping your dream in front of you (literally) is key. Creating a **vision board** or a **desire map** is perfect for the visual element. This is a simple and fun exercise in creativity. Simply create a collage of images, words and phrases that support your cravings. Then, slap it on the fridge, on your mirror in the bathroom, on your dashboard, in your cube at work, or maybe on your forehead!

Any Pinterest enthusiasts out there? Create a Pinterest board that is titled, "My Vision" and pin all those gorgeous beautiful dreams onto that board. Things you want to eat, places you want to visit, goals you want to accomplish, quotes and pictures that inspire you. A vision board created yearly in January creates a North Star in your life to follow and to guide you. The power of images seen daily can alert you to say "no" to the things that do not resonate with your intentions and a BIG Juicy YES to those things that do! Then, in December, evaluate how well you stuck to your vision and what course your life took because of your vision. Keep these boards and images where you will see them every damn day!

Below are some of the vision boards created by some of our Hot Pink Tribe at a recent Soup & Soulfood event:

STIMULATE SENSATION. Some examples of what we hear from the women who work with us, travel with us, play with us and retreat with us are: Write a book, travel abroad, take a cooking class, play the piano, leave a job, attract a partner, fall back in love with a partner, sing to an audience, create more abundance and prosperity, love really well. As you begin to gain clarity around your dreams, we challenge you to think about sensation. Ask yourself: *How will I **feel** when I achieve this?* We've all heard the tragic stories of beautiful young actresses or supermodels that appear to have it all, only to end up taking their own lives, much to our disbelief. Marilyn Monroe is a perfect example. All the fame, all the money, and all the men who desired her beauty, charm, and wit were simply not able to satiate her emotionally. All too often manifesting what we thought was a dream leaves us empty and seeking…and seeking…seeking. You are a sensory being. How you feel is truly the core of who you are. As you create that vision board or begin to map out your desires or write that life list, next to each, write down 3 words that best describe how you will FEEL when that dream is manifested. Really give this some thought, and meditate upon those feelings. It is often the feeling you believe that dream will create that is your truest desire and there may be other ways to attain that feeling. As you aim towards acting on your visions, tap into your sensations and make sure you are enjoying the journey to get to that desire. Some discomfort, yes. Torture, no.

CREATING LIVE OUT LOUD MOMENTS

"Live out loud" is a phrase we love and we use it often. We are live out loud chicks and we want to share with you what it means and how to create those moments. Somehow there is a sense that "live out loud" literally means being loud but it is actually a declaration of living a life you desire! It is about the shape, texture and quality of your life. Sometimes, it is in big life changing events and sometimes it is in the smaller moments that we truly come alive. Somehow we tend to think that moments that really shape us, bust us out and move us to new ways of living, loving, thinking and being *must* be the great big fireworks kind of moments but the truth is that what makes out loud Hot Pink moments is more about the impact that you take away from it than the event or experience itself. Certainly that trip to the other side of the world, that decision to leave a long relationship, losing a loved one, taking a job in a completely new field would all have the makings of out loud moments but it can also come in the most unexpected times and ways in small, simple moments.

> *"I was laying topless on the kitchen floor, splattered with plaster and belly laughing with my lover who was trying to carefully remove a plaster cast from my collarbone to my hip bone. We thought this might be a romantic experience but for us it turned out to be funny. I was making an art installation for Hot Pink YOUniversity and my torso, along with Christie's torso, would be displayed painted hot pink for all do see. I had intended to stand but the strips kept falling off. "Baby, you gotta lay down for me to do this," my lover told me. My first thought was, "You're kidding!*

We all know this is probably the least flattering position for our boobs...I could just see them flattening out and sliding toward my pits! He reassured me that I looked beautiful and amazing laying down too...he saw me this way and loved it!

What unfolded was unexpected and it changed me. My lover was so attentive and careful to lay and smooth the plaster strips over my body to get the best form we could which I truly appreciated. I was so totally aware of my shape in a way I hadn't been before as I knew it would be captured in sculpture. I could feel the plaster getting very warm and hardening and I was really feeling a mix of excited anticipation and yes, a bit of anxiousness as he worked to remove it.

When I returned from showering off all the leftover bits of plaster I was greeted by my cast displayed prominently propped upright in the middle of the dining table. I would like to say it was a wonderful warm fuzzy moment but in reality...it rocked me! My first thought was, "Are my boobs really that big!?" and then "I definitely have a Goddess belly!" There are positive and negative emotions behind those thoughts. What I do know is that I kept looking at my body sculpture and I began to get familiar and then started to dig it! I felt that it was a powerful and deeply moving thing to do and that I wanted to share how surreal the whole thing was. So, in this small moment in time I was truly feeling alive and oh so good in my skin as I came to love the sculpture of my female form. I can say that seeing my cast ignited as spark in me and that I live just a little more loudly and proudly since that time! This was a big Hot Pink out loud moment for me!" **~The Voice of Ann**

"*Cleaning the house is one of those things that do not feel out loud at all. My least favorites are dusting and bathrooms. However, when I clean with the music blaring and in the nude, a mundane must, turns into a hot and juicy,*

live out loud moment. There is something about nakedness that frees the mood. Other live out loud moments have been singing in front of a group of people, doesn't matter if it is not perfect, I just love to sing the song Ms. Ottis Regrets. I love driving my jeep wrangler with the top off, music full out, hair whipping around my face. On a recent trip to Atlanta to see Van Morrison, my husband and I decided to drive with the only destination in mind, Atlanta by Sunday and home for work late Monday. The rest was spontaneous and up in the air. When we met, we had kids, his and mine, and shortly thereafter created an ours. We never had that couple time to play, just jumped into bills, house, jobs and kids. Now with our kids older, we can play and explore. Our trip took us to an off the beaten track brewery and music in Mufreesboro, hot chicken in Nashville, mudding with our jeep at the Land Between the Lakes and Van Morrison in Atlanta. Fun, free, and out loud! Oh, and call before you stop over.
~The Voice of Christie

When we open ourselves to any new experiences, ways of thinking or doing things it is likely that we will find ourselves in Hot Pink out loud moments.

Our tribe had gathered for a fall weekend retreat at a gorgeous resort in beautiful Wisconsin Dells, Wisconsin. We really dove deep and challenged women to step out of their comfort zones, set intentions for some serious personal growth and open themselves to being vulnerable with others. (Of course, true to our way, there was also plenty of fun, play and laughter mixed in!) We could see throughout the weekend that Rachel was often in deep introspection and by the last day of the retreat she actually needed to take some time away. We honored and understood this was part of her journey even if we were wishing she was there for the last experiences of the weekend. A few weeks after, when doing some follow up coaching with her, she shared that a deep sadness had come over her as she opened herself to this wonderful new tribe of women and the things we were teaching. Something deep and profound had shifted in her as a result of a "great" weekend away with a kick ass tribe of women. She shared that the overwhelming thought for her was that she, "didn't want to go back home." Home to a marriage she knew was not healthy and that did not support her desires to live out loud and on fire. Now Rachel could have simply let go of the momentum she had gained in that Hot Pink retreat, fallen back into the predictable comfort of her discomfort and let go of her desires. What she did though was so completely powerful that it is a brilliant example of creating an out loud moment. Her recognition that she did not want to return home spoke to her core. Something at her core shifted and she was changed. Over the course of the next few months, she gathered her courage, clarified her needs, put a plan in place and left a twenty-plus year marriage. She got her finances in order, established her own home, gained independence, sought outside resources, grew her friendships and dove into creating the life she was so long desiring. Today, Rachel is a powerful example of the Vibe of the Hot Pink Tribe! She is living out loud and unapologetically on her terms.

Hot Pink Activity 19: Live Out Loud

Journal Prompts

- What have you done in those little ways, middle ways or great big brilliant ways to live out loud and on fire Hot Pink style!!??
- What are you wanting more of that you haven't yet honored?
- What do you desire and have yet to fulfill?
- Are you waiting for the "right" time? What/when would that be?
- This is what we know: *Now* is the right time to say a *Big* juicy *Yes* to those things that will light your fire!

RADICAL SELF-LOVE

Red hearts, lingerie, chocolate candies, roses…Ah…All this love has to start somewhere, and that somewhere is YOU! If you do not love yourself, how will others see you for the goddess you are?

"You are Hot Pink when you move from self-shame to self-love."
~Christie Gause-Bemis

Release Beliefs

One of the first things we discussed when you opened this book was about setting up an environment in our lives that is open to attracting a life of passion and joy! Letting go of beliefs that have no business showing up in your life is number one. It clears the way for attracting more of the beliefs we do want. Where did these beliefs come from? How are they currently serving you? Like sunglasses looking out onto our world, beliefs create our thoughts and that creates our feelings and that dictates our actions. Beliefs are like sunglasses looking out at the world, they change what you see, they create your reality. Two people may see the exact same scenario and both will be seen through their own lenses, shaped by their own beliefs. But, you have control over what you believe in…you can trade in your outdated sunglasses for a new pair. Look over your journals from Element I, what were some of your beliefs?

Post it somewhere to remind yourself daily that you have traded in your sunglasses for a new pair that rock! Any beliefs you had before were created by someone else's reality, by your interpretation of life experiences, the media, friends, etc. Those were all just opinions and not facts. Create what you want to believe about yourself:

What changes do you want to make? Don't get overwhelmed with the big picture…focus in on what is your next best step towards making that happen. Whether it is health goals, relationship goals, or financial goals that would support better feelings about yourself—get out of **stuck** and into the next micro-**action** towards that goal.

"Today is a great day to behave as the person
you've always wanted to be.
~Robin Sharma

It is not easy, this self-love thing. But it needs to come from within. If you always seek external validation from others for your self-worth, you will always be shackled to that person and locked into where they are at in their own lives. Let's say your partner has a bad day. The person oozing and bathing in self-love can put that into perspective, rationally think through it, and not make it about them. The person lacking self-love owns everyone's mood, everyone's bad day, and everyone's opinion. Think of the freedom that comes from being so in love with yourself?

"You is kind, You is smart, You is important."
~Aibileen Clark, The Help

Another person is allowed their moods and feelings. You are allowed your moods and your feelings. You can detach from feeling overly responsible for the unhappiness of others. Focusing on your own happiness, knowing others will do the same. Trusting.

"It gets you, or you get it!"
~Ann Murgatroyd Soe

Even if you grew up with loving messages from your primary caretakers, middle school hits, you start questioning yourself, your worth, and it is all measured by the yard stick carried by the most popular girls. We don't care how much self-love you have, it is difficult to survive some traumatic stuff as a young girl when the end goal is generally just to fit in.

Or, maybe you feel the radiant beauty of self-love until the major breakup occurs with your partner. Ouch, the rejection, the self-doubt, the feelings of worthlessness.

Or, maybe you have enjoyed the joy and exuberance of life with the one you love, who dies before you. As you move through the grief created by that void and begin to look at the future horizon, you question, "Who will love me like that again?" "At my age, how can I start over?" You start to doubt all you have to offer the next one.

Or, you face a major shift in your life. A change of any kind, and as the ground shifts beneath your once solid feet, once a stable foundation to hold you secure, your concept of self-love is put to the challenge…a career change, your grownup babies moving on by dating or moving out, all those things that fed your self-love and held it safely for you, or a move for you leaving your friends behind.

rad·i·cal adjective

1. *of or going to the* **root or origin**; *fundamental: a radical difference.*
2. *thoroughgoing or extreme, especially as regards* **change from accepted or traditional forms**: *a radical change in the policy of a company.*
3. *favoring drastic political, economic, or social reforms: radical ideas; radical and anarchistic ideologues.*
4. **forming a basis or foundation**
5. *existing* **inherently** *in a thing or person: radical defects of character.*

Source: Merriam-Webster's Learner's Dictionary

This is where the radical comes in to the concept of *radical self-love*. It is the root, it is the foundation, it is inherent. Regardless of what occurs or shifts externally, the root of our being is love for self. Like a beautiful blossoming tree that bears sweet fruit, it all begins with a healthy root system. Without that, life's shit sandwiches can shake us to the core.

> *"I am a strong believer in things don't happen to you, they happen for you. My older sister, Michelle, died of a brain tumor at the age of 29. I was 26 at the time and her death shook me to the core of my self-love. It knocked me down, but not out, of life. It was important for me to learn something about myself, about the world and take some lesson or gift away from that time. For me, I took away my strength…looking back and saying, "Are you kidding me? I survived that?!!" Not only survive but thrive after something I never thought possible to exist afterwards!"* ~*The Voice of Christie*

At our last retreat for Hot Pink YOUniversity we had an exercise what makes you a Hot Pink Woman? For each of us it is different. The following is an exercise to help form self-love for all that you are, but first we are going to share what makes each of us a Hot Pink Woman!

What makes me a Hot Pink Woman! Christie's Hot Pink Womanifesto

I accept myself for all I do and mostly for all I don't do or don't get done. I release myself from inner judgment and I teflon against the external judgers in my life…even those that may be closest to me, knowing their truth of me, is never about me, but is about where they are at in their own lives.

I am Hot Pink when I start each day anticipating fabulous new beginnings!

I accept myself, and I release self-blame, self-sabotage from my finest me and burst forward into what I "will" manifest into my greatest good.

I am Hot Pink when I move from self-shame into self-love.

I am a mom, a wife, an artist, a therapist, a writer, a daughter and a friend. I can be frazzled and overly creative with more ideas than time. I like to have fun, I like to drink some wine, to dance to laugh and I love to sing. I love to be raunchy and have an odd sense of humor at times. I love women…I love to gather women. I love to travel and feel oddly and ecstatically most myself when I am traveling. I learn more and grow more through travel as it takes me way beyond the realm of routine and comfort and into an oxymorinical discomfortable" joy. If I had to spend the rest of my life with only one message to serve to those that choose my mindful restaurant it would be to live outside of conventionality, convenience and boxes and move into YOU…however messy at times that can be, but so damn worth it!

What makes me a Hot Pink Woman!
Ann's Hot Pink Womanifesto

I AM! I am a Goddess Rising. I am a Hot Pink Woman. I choose to live from the desire to inspire and although I sometimes reflect and reminisce, I can usually be found living in the now, making my dreams my way of life. I live life out loud and on fire. I unapologetically follow my passions and purpose in life and each year is richer than the one before. I am an adventurer, gatherer, traveler, writer, lover, mentor, mother, sister, friend who sees life as an amazing journey. I live from the belief that brilliant beautiful things happen when like-minded people gather together.

I know my life purpose is to use my compassion and energy to encourage and challenge others to live in their own passion, honor others and join together in collective consciousness. I work to this purpose in all that I do and the way that I live. My life is full of juicy, wild, succulent moments and I continually spark others to create the same. I honor my unfolding. I am open to and aware of my challenges, I am willing to own my shit. I get real, raw and vulnerable. I give myself permission to make mistakes, celebrate successes, dream big and make them happen. I am a powerful bodacious "way-shower" and many have learned from the lessons I share, the stories I tell, how I show up in my relationships and how I am loving my life.

I let those close to me know just how deeply I love them with my words, sentiments and even more importantly, with my actions. Some of my greatest moments come from the journeys I take all over this great world we live in. I am truly living in a state of bliss when sharing adventures with my amazing son, my lover and true soul mate, my beloved family and friends and the powerful tribe of fellow adventurers that choose to travel the world with me.

To love me is a wild, wonderful, passionate, fun, energetic even at times frenetic ride. I am driven to let my tribe know that wherever I roam, whatever I do, I hold them always in my awareness and in my heart. I believe deeply in the clarity of the human spirit. I know there is a growing, brilliant, bold collective consciousness in our world and I am determined to be a part of that unfolding!

I view life as an endeavor of the heart and am so grateful for the opportunity to connect and grow with others and to play even just a small part in their journey to find their true personal passion, light their fire and embrace every moment life brings them! Indeed, when I am done with this lifetime I want others to say that I lived my life to its' very fullest-out loud and on fire and to honor my spirit by simply saying, "Wow! What a ride!" I am a Goddess Rising. I am a Hot Pink Woman. I AM!!!

> ### Hot Pink Activity 20: Womanifesto
>
> So, what makes you a Hot Pink Woman! **Create your own womanifesto** by asking yourself the following:
>
> - What are my strengths?
> - What are my cracks? I am referring to a concept of Wabi Sabi. Where in an asian culture there is an embrace and a celebration of cracks in pottery...so much so that in museums those cracks are filled with gold to emphasize the cracks the pottery's uniqueness, and the light is shone on it. We just love that thought!
> - When do you feel most alive? Where do you feel most alive?
> - What do you need to release about yourself and fully accept?
> - What have you overcome and what makes you strong!

Imagine being asked out on a date with that one person in your life you are most excited to share your time with. The anticipation, the thought put into your hair, your makeup, your outfit, and your attitude, your personal pep talk. Now, imagine that date is with yourself. Who more important to primp and prep for?

> *"When I turned twenty-nine, it was a milestone for me. One more foot towards 30; but, more importantly, I was now older than my big sister. She passed away the day after her 29th birthday party after a long battle with brain cancer, and here I was, alive and grateful. I always wanted a surprise birthday party and remembered the one we had given my sister for her twenty-ninth. I wondered, who, if anyone, would ever give me a surprise birthday party. I know, a weird dream from childhood. I decided that year, "why wait?". Why wait for that special someone to come into my life and throw me a party, I would do for myself.*

I sent out the invites via snail mail...long before email anyway! I had no return address and just the time, date and location. During the week leading up to the party, I would walk into unsuspecting friends, huddled in mute conversations and changing the subject as I walked into the room. It was pure joy anticipating the day of the party. On the evening of the party, I prepared the food, had drinks ready to go, and created a party atmosphere. I left a note on the door for guests to let themselves in and that the birthday girl would be arriving at 7pm. Then I donned the binoculars and parked the next street over as I watched my friends and loved ones park throughout the neighborhood and sneak up to the house. I pulled up to the house at the designated time and giggled all the way to the door, opening it to the yell of "surprise!" Love, love, love greeted me. A handful of my friends knew that there was no way my house would be that clean without me knowing something! " **~The Voice of Christie**

Why do we wait for someone to "make us happy" or to "love us in the way we desire"? It has to start with loving ourselves and treating ourselves to the pure joy life has to offer.

Love yourself radically and deeply. Love yourself first and fully. Love yourself in as many ways possible. Loving yourself to the root, the core, the foundation!

Women are caretakers and nurturers. Time to care for yourself so that you may fan the flame of others.

You may be familiar with the concept of *The Five Languages of Love* by Gary Chapman.

We use his work around this concept with couples in therapy. The Five Love Languages are: Physical Affection, Verbal Affection, Quality Time, Gifts and Acts of Service. It is about getting to know the way in which your partner feels most loved and making sure you speak his or her love language. We want you to consider what makes you feel most loved and to do that for *you*!

Physical Affection

- Move your body today…get your groove on, dance in your living room to your favorite music
- "Lotioning" spend some time spreading lotion over your body…take your time and really show your body you love it.
- Warm bath, low lights, soft music, candles…mmmmmm.
- Eat in a way your body feels good today
- Go for a walk in nature

Verbal Affection

- Look in the mirror today and say the words you wish to hear, "I love you. You are perfectly you. I enjoy you."
- Any time you are aware today of self-deprecating thoughts or words…turn that around for yourself! Lose your keys? Instead of being stupid, pause and be gentle with yourself.
- Wear something today that makes your body feel great. Look in the mirror and tell yourself just are marvelous you are.
- Today's affirmation: I can only give others as much love as I have for myself. Today I choose to love myself abundantly
- Listen to positive music today. Jana Stanfield, Karen Drucker, Karen Taylor-Good, Jen Hannah. Sing out loud!

Gifts

- Buy yourself flowers, chocolates. Stop waiting for "someone" to show you love! Give a random $10 out there today. Anonymous or not feel the joy that little gesture gives you.

- Go to the perfume counter and throw on your favorite scent. So what if you can't afford it today. At least you can smell like you can!
- Free gifts abound. Go to the library and get a romantic comedy, a favorite book. Listen to Hay House radio or watch a Tedx Talk video Googled online. Learn something inspirational.

Quality Time

- Read an inspirational book and journal to yourself about what you have read Meditate today
- Do something that you you enjoy—bowling, movies, call a friend today and make that happen go out to dinner by yourself if you are not with the love of your life…take a book and people watch. If you see other couples, draw in the loving energy they have.
- Make a list of gratitude you have today!

Acts of Service

- Get a massage today
- Write all the things you **did** accomplish today and amaze yourself
- Get a monkey off your back. If there is something weighing heavy on your mind, stop procrastinating and just get it done. You will feel better.
- Run your errands, and then treat yourself to a glass of wine or a cup of tea somewhere as a reward.
- Do a random act of kindness for someone. An anonymous Valentine's card, shoveling a neighbor's driveway, whatever you might enjoy doing. Enjoy how it elevates your energy.
- Love yourself today in a way that opens your heart to the love of another.

Love yourself. Be Compassionate. Don't say or think things about yourself that you would not even dare to say about or to another person.

THE POWER OF PLAY

Life can get so heavy and serious. We need to tap into the play. There is no "right" time for play. It is now. If you wait for all the junk in life to clear, to have all the bills paid, and relationships functioning, you will never seek the play you need. Hot Pink YOUniversity created and hosts an annual Power of Play, Summer Day Camp for Women. It is a day of play where we dress up, have a photo booth with silly costumes, play swearing croquet (just like when we were kids and saying swear words was naughty fun), paint, and create a wild rumpus down the road in our costumes. What is the point? Just *Fun*! No other deep, worldly intentions. It is to just have fun with our girlfriends.

The power of play is rooted in science. Laughter is healing. It is a cardio workout. It releases bad chemicals and creates good ones. Why deny our bodies what it needs to function. Have some fun! Forget the kids! We encourage you to create your own play dates with girlfriends.

> *"The weeks, and then days, leading up to the Power of Play Summer Camp, I had some reservations about going to an event where I really didn't know anyone. Would I fit in? Would I connect with anyone else there? Would I embarrass myself? It turned out to be the most fun and carefree day I've had as an adult! We dressed up and acted silly, played some yard games, ran a lemonade stand to raise money for cancer patients, ate our dinner on butcher paper, and felt totally free to let our inner kid come out to play! The absolute best part of the day for me was taking a small empty box and writing or drawing pictures of things that hold us back in our lives. At the end of the day, as we were sitting around the campfire, we took*

turns talking about all the things we felt were holding us back from really enjoying life. Some of the things I shared were my health issues, being overweight, worrying about what others think of me, taking on too much responsibility. We then threw our boxes into the fire and watched as those negative thoughts burned away! We shared a lot of laughter and just a few tears, and I left with a feeling of sisterhood and belonging! Thank you, Ann and Christie for a most awesome and inspiring day I'll never forget!"
~The Voice of Firestarter, Barb Sabatine

Many of us feel depleted. We feel too adult-like. Why be so serious all the time? What does this serve for us in life? How does this infect our relationships?

Madison residents, Jason and Kim Kotecki have created an entire business and livelihood around this concept, and they call it Escape Adulthood. They have created the term Adultitis and have a quiz you can take and cures to create more childlike play in life. How do you know if you have contracted Adultitis you can take their quiz here: http://escapeadulthood.com/blog/

Hot Pink Activity 21:
We have created our own Hot Pink Test
for women who take life much too seriously.
Take the quiz below to see:

Part I: True or False

1. You have eaten your lunch at your desk, car or cubicle in the last month? True or False
2. You have spent your lunch break in the room talking about work, complaining about work or stress, or your marriage or your coworkers? True or False
3. You have mainly used water for bathing or cleaning and not for playing, splashing, frolicking under? True or False

Ignite Your Life

4. You can't remember the last time you read a book for pleasure? True or False
5. Your idea of "shaking your thang" is your head, no? True or False
6. You're not sure if you even have a "your thang"! True or False

Total your how many are true.

Mark that total here:_____

Part II: Read the following list determine how often you've done them in the last month. (Rate them according to: Never 5, Once or twice 3, Often 0)

1. Picked up a paintbrush _____
2. Shut off your phone for 24 hours_____
3. Shut off your computer for 24 hours_____
4. Blew a bubble_____
5. Danced_____
6. Played with a hula hoop_____
7. Sang off or on key_____
8. Splashed in water_____
9. Got mud on yourself…on purpose!_____
10. Laughed until your sides hurt_____
11. Played dress-up_____
12. Played catch_____
13. Tagged someone and yelled "You're IT!"_____
14. Slept in_____
15. Delighted in a sunset_____
16. Had a lemonade stand_____
17. Told stories around a campfire _____
18. Played a musical instrument_____
19. Had fun! Simple, abundant, juicy *fun*!_____
20. Always need an alarm to get up_____?
21. You use the words "overwhelmed," "stressed out," and/or "I am tired" weekly?_____

You operate on autopilot most days?_____

Write your total here:_____

Now total the two parts of the quiz here:_____

If you scored:

73 to 116 Serious case of "Way too serious!". Time for a Hot Pink Intervention!

50-72 Moderate case of overwhelm and overload. If you do not do something soon, it could turn into a serious case. Relearn how to play again. Share a laugh with a girlfriend.

21-49 Seriousness is beginning to creep up in your life. Time to revisit your pleasure list and self-love list and create some space and time for those activities.

20 and under…Ummmmmm, *You* rock, Sista! and you are just the kind of women we want to play with! Come and teach us what you know oh most wise and delicious *One*!

The bottom line: Play is essential. Schedule a play date today with someone. Schedule a play date with yourself!

Element IV: Be A Firestarter--Spark Others!

Ahhhhh…just breath! As we enter into our last Hot Pink Element. The changes you have undertaken to this point, all beautiful, hot, juicy and bursting open at the seams. It would appear that you are done at this point. Having made your own transformation, you feel complete. Element IV is not just snuck in there to make this book thicker. It is an essential Element that we believe passionately about. Hot Pink YOUniversity believes that we all need to have one another's backs in this world. That once you have transformed, it is essential that you plug into a powerful tribe of sister friends, soul sisters who build you up.

That is one part of Element IV, building your personal Hot Pink Tribe, joining our larger Hot Pink Tribe. Another part of this Element is being the spark to others in two ways. One way is to encourage the growth, the language and narrative of other women, the knowledge you have acquired through this book and through your own experiences. That is the primary reason we wrote this book. It takes grit to write a book…it is not all pleasure and fluff looking beautiful at the computer and eating cake. It is long hours of editing, creating and then more editing and creating. Why do we do it? Because it is our purpose. It is our spark to anyone whose hands wrap around this book and take it to read.

The second part of being the spark to others is on an even larger scale. Are you ready for this? What if all women growing, encouraging, laughing, sharing, finding pleasure, supporting one another actually heals the hurts that are in the world? We believe that women and the feminine power, the way we are wired and think has deep healing powers for the world. Our feminine energy of flow, social connections, empathy centers and ability to multi-task is so important during this intense time of conflict, shifting perspective, and disconnect.

This seems like a lofty endeavor. Hot Pink YOUniversity is just one small piece in the vast puzzle of the overall solution. There are other feminine energy oriented movements. And, it does not discount the masculine energy that is needed. The pendulum of need has shifted however to need the feminine at this moment in history.

> "The world will be saved by the Western woman."
> ~Dalai Lama, 2009 World Peace Summit

Think about the women out there, suffering, in pain, making the same choices in life and expecting different outcomes.

Your co-workers that complain and rumble all day long. Your family members that we so easily label or cut off or write off. What if living our life fully inspired or impacted a shift in them? We love when women feel the shift and then invite women to our events. That is the biggest compliment we can receive. The trust in what we do rippling out to other women. When you are done with this book share with a sister friend in need, let the ripple begin!

THE ART AND SCIENCE OF HOT PINK RELATIONSHIPS

A Hot Pink Sister Friend is:

- Not afraid to sparkle bright and leaves a little sparkle wherever she goes
- Unapologetic in her abundance and when able and willing to, shares that with all her other sister friends in a way that moves others to join and manifest their own abundance
- A Firestarter…when she comes into her own radiance, she calls back to her sister friends and the dark and says, "Get the hell over here with me! It's amazing!"

Sparks others to live a life on fire!

We have been inspired by others along the way. We did not come into this Hot Pink life alone, but lead by other Hot Pink Sister friends. Sister friends who felt so grounded in their own lives, that they knew what it took to pull others forward along the way. Sister friends who did not feel in competition with us, but in collaboration and reverence. We are social creatures desiring a human connection desiring to be loved, to matter and to find our tribe. This Element is all about continuing to honor your truth in the company of others. Finding a tribe of sisterhood that is positive and affirming, wants you to succeed and to be the best you can possibly be in this life. This is what it means to be a Firestarter!

THE VIBE OF THE HOT PINK TRIBE

"Oh, there's something about the women in my life."
~Holly Near

Oh, to luxuriate in change, to bathe and back paddle through the Hot Pink Life you have created as you moved through this process of creating your Hot Pink Life. It feels good to feast at the banquet table of life. And you are not done yet. Feasting at the banquet of life requires a group of women, a tribe to join you in laughter and celebration, joy and gratitude. A tribe of beautiful women joining you in glorious change.

It is so important to cultivate the vibe of *You*r tribe. We are all in this together—having one another's backs, celebrating our triumphs, holding us up in our depths in life, encouraging and connecting. Let's take a little glimpse in this area…

Hot Pink Activity 22: Vibe of the Tribe Assessment

Fill in the name of a friend (you can use the name of a girlfriend more than once)

A friend that makes you pee your pants with laughter_____
A friend that touches your soul_____
A friend that is your constant_____
A friend that listens deeply_____
A friend that helps you celebrate_____

> A friend who honors your abundance_____
> A friend that takes personal responsibility for who she is, how she got there, and where she is heading next_____
> A friend who is fun_____
> A friend who admires you_____
> A friend you admire back_____
> A friend you can admit your secrets to, with no judgments_____
>
> How many friends were you able to come up with as you filled this out? Did you have any blank spaces?

We shared earlier with you the quote by American Entrepreneur Jim Rohn, "We are the average o the five people we spend the most time with." If it is true how is your average? There are no handicaps given here. It lies with you to take responsibility for that average.

If it is high, congrats-a-fuckin'-lations! You rock. You glow and illuminate like moths drawn to a flame, your sisters come to you. Because you radiate life, life comes back to you. Celebrate that and spark others around you to celebrate that too!

So, so and average…fill in the gaps baby. Couldn't think of a friend that makes you pee your panties from laughing? We all need one of those and you simply must go out and seek that. Humor, laughter are the essentials in life. Laughter is healthy for your mind, body and soul. Couldn't find a friend that honors your abundance? In a world where we are taught competition is good and success is everything, it is abso-fuckin-lutely important to have a friend that does not writhe with green envy in her eyes, but your light makes her light shine brighter and she knows it! These are the friendships we need ladies!

How low can you go? This is not the limbo at the roller rink. It is time to dig deep and move that average up a significant notch. And that is just what we will do!

The Hot Pink Tribe of *Your* Vibe!

> *"Lots of people want to ride with you in the limo,*
> *but what you want is someone who will take*
> *the bus with you when the limo breaks down."*
> *~Oprah Winfrey*

Examining our Sisterhood Now

"It wasn't until my late twenties that I seriously knew how to be in a relationship with a woman. Growing up, I had two best friends in high school who were girls and my relationships were predominantly with boys. They were easier. I could navigate those relationships better. If you disagreed with a boy, you got it out there and then it was done and over. But, girls…it dragged on and you had to navigate those waters, differently each time. Too many rules, too many emotions, it was overwhelming to me and I was not good at it.

I was bullied by a girl in the seventh grade, junior high, and witnessed other girls throughout grade school and junior high being bullied as well. It shaped me. Science even says whether we are bullied or the witness to bullying, we change the neural connections in our brain due to the trauma of bullying. I know that this is true in how I felt about myself and the world. Girls scared me. What they could make me feel and how they could bring to the surface those most vulnerable and negative beliefs about myself.

*After my divorce in my mid-twenties, I knew how much I needed sisterhood. Since I was shy, I had always relied on my big sister, Michelle. After her death, that was not possible and my friends from high school had moved away or were busy with their own lives and I had a **lot** of time when my son was with his dad." ~**The Voice of Christie***

It is essential for our spirit and our fire-filled lives to have sisterhood. We feed one another estrogen energy and deep belly laughs as only women can.

Sometimes it is through our discomfort that we are motivated to make a change. If the assessment above made you uncomfortable, that is okay…let's work with that reality and create a new story.

Hot Pink Keys to Sisterhood:

KEY #1: You have to create it!

It does not show up naturally in life like the sun rising and setting, it must be cultivated into your life.

> *"I loved to read books, book clubs were becoming a big hit, thanks to Oprah. So I started a book club. I put up flyers at work. I sent them to a few of my relatives whom I knew liked to read, and in 1998, I began with a small group of women strangers and created Changing Chapters Book Club. Many of the core beginners still meet today, and there are many new faces that have joined us as well. We have become best friends who laugh, travel, and support one another in our joys and sorrows. Now with sixteen members, I am amazed with how we positively are there for one another." ~The Voice of Christie*

What are some natural interest that you have? Snowshoeing, reading, knitting, rock-climbing? Is there a club or group in your area that has this? If not, create it. Talk to others, come out of your shell, get out of your comfort zone and spark the excitement in others. It all begins with one. If not you, then who!? If not now, then when!?

Put yourself out there. New friendships are not going to be created by sitting at home, watching more TV, or whatever else you busy yourself with, but on being out there living a life out loud and on fire!

Strike up a conversation—Just do it!

We want you to find the very next stranger in your life and just strike up a random conversation with that person. Even if this is not going to be your new BFF, this person will be your practice for the next one.

Share of yourself—through our stories, we as women, uniquely connect.

Think back to that assessment. Think of coworkers, relatives, old friends who may be potential candidates for creating a Hot Pink Tribe of your own! Make one gesture in the next twenty-four hours towards reconnecting with that person. If you feel the fear of rejection, go back to element one and reread!

Key #2: We are all in this together

We all feel self-doubt. We all approach others with caution and fear. Some friendships may not work out, some may fit into our life for a time and then we grow apart. But, just like dating our significant others, we need to put ourselves out there with friendships and realize we are all going through some of the same things.

Connect. Create. Imagine. Laugh.
A shirt created for a group of women taking our workshop Creating a Hot Pink Work Environment, 2012

There is a scene in *Desperate Housewives*, where Lynette, mother of three, is slowly crashing and burning in life. She has become overworked as a house mom, her bratty kids are testing her patience, and, in order to maintain her energy to "get it all done," she has turned to her kids Ritalin. At the end of her rope, she walks her kids to the neighbors, looking like a crazy woman, leaves them there and then goes to the park to cry. There, her girlfriends find her and take turns sharing stories of their own. Mommy stories when we just lose it! We crash, we burn, we feel we are the only ones getting this thing called life wrong, and we feel alone. We share the stories of our crash, our perfectly imperfect lives, we bond, connect, and are real. So, yes, we need to share, the good, the bad, the ugly. Sharing is different than complaining. Refer back to the Hot Pink Tongue. We don't want to create a tribe of whiney, bitchy, complainers, but, a real tribe of feminine energy and connection as our stories unfold with one another to learn and feel like we are in this together.

What stories do you hold close to you for fear of judgment? What stories make you uniquely *You **that you are bursting forward waiting to be*** shared with other women?

Awareness, my reality

Now that we have done some work on building that awareness of what is and what we desire to be. It is time to shine that mirror back in your face and take a check into your reality? Who am I? And, how am I showing up in relationships? How do I want my tribe to make me feel? And, how do I want others to feel in my presence?

Key #3: You have to Show Up in a relationship

> *"When I went on my first "voluntour" trip in 2010 with Jana Stanfield and a group of twenty-nine complete strangers, I traveled by myself. No other friend or relative*

joined me. I just went. I met up with the group in the Los Angeles airport waiting for our international flight to Vietnam. Through two weeks of traveling in a foreign country, you learn to rely on one another. It also allowed me to see for the first time, at the age of forty, how to have deeply connected and intimate conversations with others. In my book, the Busy Woman's Retreat, I talk about the MMMmmmmm Moment I witnessed on that trip. Where people would have these conversations and at some point have this deep pleasurable look on their faces and just "hmmmmm" at one another. I never experienced these heart moments as most of my conversations growing up took place over busy hands: while mom rolled out a pie crust, or over dinner shoveling food, or driving a car. I did not have many MMMmmmmm moments in my life and when I came home from that trip, I deepened my listening, I used my new skill of tapping into a person's energy and my relationships improved significantly. We have to be there in the moment with a person, idle hands and open heart!" ~**The Voice of Christie**

Focus on the person. Be in that moment in time and tap into the heart energy of the other person. Create a beautiful Mmmmm Moment. Your relationships will deepen. Focus on being in there **towards** that person versus **for** that person.

The basis for any healthy relationship is when we do not take responsibility for others, but towards others. You know that you are overdoing, enabling or co-dependent when:

When I am responsible for others I…

- Fix, caretake, protect, make things better
- Feel exhausted, anxious, tired, angry and frustrated
- Manipulate the circumstances
- Hide what I am truly feeling
- Control the outcome, or at least attempt to Steal life's lessons from other people

- Focus on the solution and outcome
- Don't establish healthy boundaries for self, as you don't know if that will lead to problems in the relationship
- And, you know that you are cultivating healthy friendships and relationships when you:

When I am responsible towards others…

- Sympathize, empathize, support as I can and am able and willing to
- Feel at peace, relaxed, deepened sense that all will be well
- Allow the circumstances to unfold as they need to
- Express my true feelings and thoughts in caring ways
- Recognize what is within my control (which is often very little) and release what is not mine to control.
- Allow that person to grow at the pace he or she needs to.
- Focus on the journey along the way.
- Establish my own healthy boundaries of how I desire to be treated.

Key #4: Speak your truth

Often women can dominate over one another. You need to tap into your needs and check in with yourself…do I want that? What do I need from this friendship? What is hurting me? What do I need to stay away from? And voice that in your friendships. It may not always lead to change, but then you know and you have honored yourself and your needs.

> *"By history, I would often not "speak my truth" when in conflictual situations in hopes of not hurting feelings, having the person upset with me, or adding to the already active situation. I would easily take on their feelings, be apologetic and generally feeling responsible. This often*

left me with unresolved feelings of hurt, frustration, unrealistic guilt and being used or taken for granted. This conflict avoidance also contributed to a pattern of the other person's needs/feelings somehow being more important than mine, and gave the message that I was all good with/perhaps even agreed with the things they were saying. This is not totally Hot Pink! Some years back, I found myself in a friendship circumstance with a woman who presented and lived in the world in a way that came across initially as gentleness and softness which was appealing. It eventually became quite clear that it was more of a victim pattern of vulnerability there was reactivity, projection, mistrust and fear behind much of what she did and how she handled life circumstances. When several situations didn't end up the way she believed they should, I found myself being criticized, scolded, and even having my integrity questioned. In the past, I would have been crushed by this level of conflict. In this situation I was able to find the courage and the clarity to stand firm in my sense of the situation, my truth, and my values. I didn't take on any of what was obviously much more related to her own life circumstance, fears, choices, etc. Even though she was coming at me with a lot of hurtful negativity, I was clear in my choices, honored my right to make decisions and was unapologetic in my message to her. She was expecting me to feel responsible FOR her and I was only willing to be responsible TO her. I listened without defending or taking on what she was expressing and then I spoke my truth! It felt great! I left that meeting feeling compassion or her journey without taking on anything that was not mine. This was such a Hot Pink moment for me! I also decided to leave the relationship with a clear conscience, a stronger sense of self, a validation that I am able to practice what I teach and a hope that she would learn what was necessary for her from this experience. Initially, I felt some sadness, disappointment and grief which is natural. What didn't I feel? I didn't feel guilty or bad or over responsible or resentful. I found my voice and spoke my truth. I felt free, courageous and strong!" ~**The Voice of Ann**

Dr. Brene Brown talks about six women friends with whom we do not want to share our shame story. To watch her powerful talk with Oprah: http://www.youtube.com/watch?v=s8Pp7QB-6GrE It illustrates the power that another women can have over how we feel about ourselves, our stories, and our truth. If you know your truth, speak it. It can be spoken with eloquence and class if you so choose.

Key #5: Honor that woman

Not just to her face, but behind her back. No gossip or passive-aggressive communication, but compassion and understanding for the other person and the shoes she has worn in this lifetime. Remember when you were creating your life story and your events that shaped you, your limiting beliefs and toxic messages? She has that same experience too. She has a story. She has limiting beliefs and toxic messages. She has seen shit and has had shit happen too!

When we gossip about someone else, it reflects much more of who we are as a person, not so much on the truth of that woman. When we stop our own judgments and assumptions or mind-reading about others, our own lives get freer and clearer. One of the best ways to stop worrying about what others may be thinking about you, is to stop your judgmental thoughts of others.

Let this be a gossip, judgment free day. When you notice your head thinking about what another woman is doing, wearing, *Stop*! Say to yourself, "Not my business!" and just observe without judgment. Listen with the depth of "Mmmmmm" as we shared above in Christie's story, be in that moment as much as possible.

Key #6: Know your boundaries

And honor them. We would love to get to a place on this earth where there is no need for boundaries. Where we show up and exude pure love like that baby clean slate of our birth. But, until that happens we need boundaries to keep our integrity safe. If a woman regularly brings out your negative qualities or baggage, you need to examine that relationship and what it may be able to bring you. There may be limits to that relationship. We need friends to laugh with, to be serious with, to cry, to just breath with. There is a purpose to all of our relationships and no **one** relationship can bring us all we need to feel our energy. Take what you can get from relationships while still honoring your boundaries.

What are some of our boundaries in friendships? Think back to a time when you felt angry or hurt or resentful in your relationships. It probably can help shed some light on a boundary that you have or need to have.

Possible Boundaries to have in a relationship:

- Be on time for me.
- If you say you are going to do _____, I need you to follow through and be consistent.
- I need you to listen, when or if I need advice, I will promise to let you know. But, if I don't, just *Be* for me.
- No judging me and I will do the same for you.
- Have my damn back!
- Go deep and let's be real.
- I don't care what car you drive, what you make for a living, what kind of house you live in or who you know, I just want to hang, be real and be us.
- Give me unconditional love and positive regard.
- Don't make me feel like spending time with me is an obligation or something you are fitting into your schedule, but a desire to play and have fun.
- Let's spark one another.

Key #7: Spark, Inspire, Radiate

When we have found our true selves and are living in our fire, we spark those around us. Here is a story of a Firestarter living out loud and sparking others:

Laurie was living a life of fairly social isolation and routine. having dealt with the loss of her husband years prior, she had pretty much lived in her comfort zone. Lonely for the company of others she began attending some Hot Pink Events and Playshops. She learned about herself, her loss and finding a place of unconditional positive acceptance of the Hot Pink Tribe. She began creating her own outings, taking a risk by asking a new friend to lunch or to stop over for a fire. Soon, she began introducing other women into her tribe and connecting women with one another, knowing at these two people needed to connect because they had something in common. To watch Laurie grow over the course of a year with Hot Pink YOUniversity has been amazing; the connections she has made and the people she has inspired and sparked along the way. She connected with Hot Pink YOUversity with her friend Carla who runs a grassroots, nonprofit organization named Spare Change. Spare Change meets monthly and women bring $25 to the meeting. At that meeting, stories are presented by others in the community needing a helping hand. A woman in a shelter looking to get her car fixed so she can find a job, first month's rent, clothes for an interview, you name it. Well, because of that connection, Hot Pink YOUniversity was given a generous donation to their Women's Warrior Foundation. This fund is local and helps women going through cancer treatment to feel beautiful. Spa treatments, wigs, nails and makeup. One woman, Laurie, introduced another woman, who changed the lives of many women…now that is a Hot Pink Spark moment! That is true Hot Pink Sisterhood! That is the Vibe of the Hot Pink Tribe!

And there are many more stories like this out there!

The Vibe of the Hot Pink Tribe

These women, Laurie and Carla, ooze what it is all about to inspire and spark others. Once we get our mojo, that mojo will only grow and radiate brighter if we give it to others. Pay it forward ladies and imagine what we can do here!

"Amazing things happen when women gather together."
~Sue Monk Kidd

LIVING YOUR HOT PINK PURPOSE!

Purpose
n. noun

- the reason why something is done or used : **the aim or intention** of something
- the feeling of **being determined** to do or achieve something
- the aim or goal of a person : what a person is trying to do, **become**, etc.
- Source: Merriam-Webster's Learner's Dictionary

When we step into our purpose we are creating a legacy, fulfilling our destiny. A legacy, something handed down to the next generation, to the next tribe of sisterhood, to our families, to our friends. Our destiny, is a predetermined aim for our life, sometimes beyond our human control. It pulls at us and draws us in, like a moth to a flame. When we are not living our destiny, we feel unbalanced, dissonance internally. Oprah Winfrey talks so profoundly in this interview that we invite you to watch before going any further (copy and paste in your browser): https://www.youtube.com/watch?v=kKvcNYzkip4

Oprah talks about knowing there is something more for you, a gut feeling. What gut feeling do you have for you higher purpose, your life's work?: Oprah says that if you are in a bad relationship, you are a student of a good relationship. What are you a "student" of:

> "Find a way to express your truth or
> you are not living your fullest life."
> ~Oprah

When we are living and breathing our life's purpose, whatever this may be we do it regardless of ego. Meaning it does feed us to be recognized by others, to be able to "show off" (which is not necessarily a bad thing!!!), but that we do that life purpose activity or service because to not do it would be impossible. Oprah does what she does, receives a multitude of recognitions and kudos for it, but the essence of what she does comes from a drive, a need, an impossibility to not do what she does.

> *"If you do not live the life you believe,*
> *you will soon believe the life you live."*
> *~Unknown*

In Element II and III, we encouraged you to say big, hot juicy *Yes's*! For many of you…that may also coincide and mirror something that is *Your* Life's Purpose! That *Yes* could be that ripple you create in the world. *Wow*…take that in! Sit with that for a moment and ask yourself, "how is my big *Yes* also a piece of my life's purpose?"

> *"You can't just visualize and go eat a sandwich."*
> *~Jim Carrey*

Hot Pink Activity 23: My Hot Pink Purpose

Find your 2-3 favorite qualities, strengths, abilities about yourself:

Ask 5 friends, colleagues or co-workers your strengths or qualities:

> What verbs are your favorite ways of expressing those parts of yourself:
>
> If the world were a better place, if everyone were living a hot pink life in the way you see it, what would be happening, what would be occurring around you? How would people be feeling about themselves? How would people be treating one another?
>
> What are some of the wabi-sabi, flaws or imperfect ways you show up in the world?

Christie's Hot Pink Process:

> *Creativity and Zest for life, people listen when I speak*
> *To inspire and To support/gather*

*Everyone is living their passions and purpose. Everyone is thinking in a global capacity. Everyone is supportive and encouraging each other. There is abundance for **Everyone!***

My imperfections are disorganized and cluttered, can get impatient.

My Hot Pink Life's Purpose is to use my creativity and zest for life, as well as influence over others, to inspire and support and gather others to live with passion and purpose in a global thought capacity, being supportive and encouraging one another along their unique journeys in absolute abundance! And I forgive myself for the clutter, disorganization and impatient that desire creates. Loving that it makes the way I do this purpose unique and with the goal in mind.

What does this mean for me? Everything—all the movements I make, decisions I create, are an evolution of this course in my life—my destiny, my legacy. And, I attract others who manifest the same.

Living Your Hot Pink Purpose!

Ann's Hot Pink Process:

Compassionate and Energetic, passionate and pleasure seeking
To encourage and To Challenge
Everyone is living in their passions, honoring each other, and joining together in collective consciousness
My wabi-sabi is impatience and at times intense in how I feel

My purpose is to use my compassion and energy, pleasure seeking and passion to encourage and challenge others to live in their passion, honor others and join together in collective consciousness. Fully embracing my impatience and intense emotions that come from this.

"We are sitting at a waterfront restaurant in Hayward, Wisconsin, called Waterfront, and talking about this concept of **Reclaiming Your Purpose**. Christie: To lead people to see in more global ways. Our impact over the world, our ripple effect. My Indulgent "Why": Makes our own pain seem so small. Ann: To live in the passion I feel when I am a "way-shower" and inspiring others. My Indulgent "Why"—Reconnects to an old energy, keeps me in my passion. This talk makes me think, 'what does the world need from me? If I were at the end of my life, what would make me feel "used up," in gratitude?'"
~*The Voice of Ann*

"Life should not be a journey to the grave with the intention of arriving safely in a pretty and well preserved body, but rather to skid in broadside in a cloud of smoke, thoroughly used up, totally worn out, and loudly proclaiming "Wow! What a Ride!"
~Hunter S. Thompson

In Element I, you got rid of limiting beliefs, those things we no longer need or want to believe in about ourselves. And, you created some new and power-filled beliefs. You put on your Hot Pink Big Girl Panties and took full ownership of your life, your choices, and your future.

When you are living your Life Purpose you are:

- Learning new skills
- Having new experiences
- Feeling alive and on fire
- Opening yourself to new possibilities
- Connecting to your Indulgent Why's
- And more!

Let's end by breaking this down for you!

Re-read your life purpose statement above. Share this with five other people in the next week. By claiming it and verbalizing it, you are owning it and now accountable to it: Post on Facebook and somewhere in your home and work environment: "I am a stand for my life's purpose which is…(your life's purpose statement).

Level One of Reclaiming *Your* Life's Purpose, Hot Pink and Effortless:

This level is effortless. It will take you into creating daily habits for yourself, small steps towards achieving this and mini-mindshifts. What is a small step or shift you could do to create your Life's Purpose?

Example: I could read books about topics pertaining to global issues and be more informed of how I could help others.

Level Two of Reclaiming *Your* Life's Purpose, Hot Pink and Effort-ful:

This level is full on and in action. It is talkin' the talk and now walkin' the walk! Woohoo! What big YES can you make to fully step into your Life's Purpose? What time frame do you see for yourself in achieving these things?

Example: I am going to start a company called Hot Pink YOUniversity so that I can co-create with others in thinking more globally and have fun and abundance while doing this. My time frame is 3-5 years with steps towards achieving this mindfully carried out weekly and gradually growing.

Level Three, Oh My Fucking God. This is Hot Pink!
This is full throttle, scares you, and moves you and others around you in big and juicy ways! Leaps and jumps to your Hot Pink Life's Purpose. C'mon ladies. What could this be for you?

Example: I am going to ask to do a workshop in Turkey with my business partner, then see how I can incorporate traveling for free and bring other women and men I adore to go with me. So they can shift and grow and think on more global terms doing good for others.

Assess what level you are ready to live your Hot Pink Purpose. Let us know how we can support that! Another challenge we give to women is to create their own eulogy. What legacy would you want to leave? What would you want to be remembered for?

YOU ARE A WOMAN ON FIRE!

You **did it!!**

Give yourself a great big, juicy Brag! Celebrate! You have finished just one of the many succulent adventures. that Hot Pink YOUniversity has to offer! *You* have kicked up your game and are on your way to being a Firestarter! Thank you for joining us. *You* are on your way to the Art and Science of Living Life on Fire. *You* are on becoming your true Hot Pink Self. *Congratulations!*

"GODDESS RISING"

The song of the crow rises calling me out.
I slide through the narrow slit in the door and the amber rays of sunrise hit my cheek.
I turn just in time to see the crow take flight from familiar rooftop perch.
He calls to me and I now see myself now as I thrust forward out and away from all that once was.
The water waits for me-glass in motion, undulating cerulean heaven sky.
I move with abandon to the shore as pieces of my world fall away from me.
I step to water's edge scraped raw from the departure of who I once was.
I stand long, languid, naked and sway to the rhythm of Mother Earth oozing from the crystalline sands under my feet.
I reach to the heat of the sunrise and push strong into the brilliant sparkling water.
I feel the rush as I am swallowed into the depths, shedding all, skin alive and electric.
I dive into this fluid amniotic and birth myself.
Goddess emerges dripping in the jewels of water and sun.
Standing tall in my power I throw my head back, feel the heat of the sun and know to where it is that I have come.
I allow the sound to come to and through me.
I call out to all that I am reborn from earth to water, water and again earth.
The crow answers with one last piercing cry and I too spread my wings and fly.

*Please do not use or reproduce for any reason other than personal use without permission of author Ann Murgatroyd-Soe

RESOURCES BY THE ELEMENT

Element I:

Books
Schieck, Rochelle (2016). *Qoya: A Compass for Navigating an Embodied Life that is Wise, Wild and Free.* Inspire & Move LLC.
Northrup, Kate (2013). *Money, A Love Story: Untangle Your Financial Woes and Create the Life You Really Want.* Hay House, Inc.
Cameron, Julia (2011). *The Prosperous Heart: Creating a Life of "Enough".* New York, NY: The Penguin Group.
Money Blogtalk with Hot Pink YOUniversity:
Aired August 22, 2014. *Financing Your Passions Getting Clear on Your Money with Hot Pink YOUniversity.* Retrieved from: http://www.blogtalkradio.com/hotpinkyou/2014/08/22/financing-your-passions-getting-clear-on-your-money-with-hot-pink-youniversity
Aired 2014. *Part Two: Financing Your Passions Hot Pink YOUniversity Money Talk.* Retrieved from: http://www.blogtalkradio.com/hotpinkyou/2014/09/08/part-two-financing-your-passions-hot-pink-youniversity-money-talk

SARK Books

Songs
Fight Song by Rachel Platten
Roar by Katy Perry

Element II:

Hicks, Esther and Hicks, Jerry (2004). *Ask and It Is Given: Learning to Manifest Your Desires.* Hay House, Inc.

Ortner, Nick (2013). *The Tapping Solution: A Revolutionary System for Stress-Free Living.* Hay House.

Mama Gena's School of Womanly Arts: *http://www.mamagenas.com/*

Jana Stanfield and Travel with Jana: *http://www.janastanfield.com/voluntour-with-jana/*

Songs:
Something More by Sugarland

Element III:

Attwood, Chris and Bray Attwood, Janet (2007). The Passion Test: The Effortless Path to Discovering Your Destiny. New York, NY: The Penguin Group.

Chapman, Gary (2015). *The Five Love Languages: The Secret to Love That Lasts.* Northfield Publishing

Ayurvedic Massage: Abhyanga *Retrieved from YouTube: https://www.youtube.com/watch?v=_HQLsfZh5js*

Kotecki, Jason W. (2005). *Escape Adulthood: 8 Secrets from Childhood for the Stressed-Out Grown-Up.* JBiRD INK, Ltd.

Songs:
Roar by Katy Perry (again, because we can!)
Karen Drucker, Karen Taylor-Good, Jen Hannah
If I Were Brave and No Fear by Jana Stanfield

Element IV:

Brown, Dr. Brene' (March 2013). *6 Types of People Who Do Not Deserve to Hear Your Shame Story.* Super Soul Sunday, Own Network. Retrieved from: *https://www.youtube.com/watch?v=s8Pp7QB6GrE.*

HOT PINK ACTIVITIES

Element I: Page #

Activity 1:	Panty Raid	24
Activity 2:	Igniting Limitless Beliefs	27
Activity 3:	Hot Pink Relationship Boundaries	28
Activity 4:	Hot Pink Responsibility and Ownership	32
Activity 5:	Self-Love Jar	33
Activity 6:	Money Relationships	35-36
Activity 7:	Money Must Do's	37-38
Activity 8A:	Victim Letter	46
Activity 8B:	I Forgive You Letter	47
Activity 8C:	Gratitude Letter	48
Activity 9:	Hot Pink Receiving	52
Activity 10:	Gift, Receive, & Ask	56

Element II:

Activity 11:	Want and More Mindshifts	59
Activity 12:	Want and More Words	61-62
Activity 13:	Pleasure 101	66
Activity 14:	Personal Pleasure Principle	67-68
Activity 15A:	Old Stories	79
Activity 15B:	Your New "*Hot Pink*" Stories	81
Activity 16:	Embrace Your Shape	90

Element III:

Activity 17:	Dream Big	101
Activity 18:	Comfort Zones	105
Activity 19:	Live Out Loud	112
Activity 20:	Womanifesto	119

Element IV:

Activity 21:	Hot Pink Play Test	125-127
Activity 22:	Vibe of the Tribe Assessment	131-132
Activity 23:	My Hot Pink Purpose	145-146

HOT PINK YOUNIVERSITY

If your juices are flowing, you are loving the Vibe of our Hot Pink Tribe and you are ready to create a life of passion, purpose and play we are ready and waiting to introduce you to ALL that Hot Pink YOUniversity has to offer. We offer speaking engagements, playshops, intensive, play retreats and camps, and immersive travel experiences. Here are just a few of the ways you can play with Ann and Christie through Hot Pink YOUniversity:

- Learn the 7 Steps to Reignite Passion, Purpose and Play into your life.
- Have more intimate, intensive, exclusive VIP time at events and playshops and
- Travel the world with Hot Pink YOUniversity
- Have access to personal mentoring, small groups, even one-on-one time with the Bodacious Broads of Hot Pink YOUniversity
- Learn to live Out loud and On Fire
- Be ready and want to embrace all that is YOU…the good, the not so good and everything in between
- Create a life that is fulfilling all YOUr wishes, wants, dreams and desires
- Find balance and honor YOUrself equally with others in YOUr life.
- Expand YOUr tribe
- Bring the amazing energy of Hot Dudes into your life…in whatever ways YOU desire.
- Live succulent and juicy…sharing YOUr spark to ignite others

- Become that turned on woman that turns on the YOUniverse!

Join our mailing list at: www.hotpinkyou.com
Like us on Facebook at: Hot Pink YOUniversity
Questions? Comments? Testimonials? Contact us at: hotpinkyou@gmail.com

ANN MURGATROYD-SOE MSSW, LCSW

Ann is a licensed psychotherapist with over 20 years of experience and co-owner of Central WI Counseling Associates, a private psychotherapy practice. She was born into a culturally diverse family that has given her a deep appreciation for diversity and an interest in multiple spiritual belief systems. Several life changing experiences lead Ann to expand her practice beyond traditional health and wellness models. Ann has her bachelor's and master's degree from the University of Wisconsin-Madison. She has hosted and facilitated numerous wellness and women's retreats. She lectures for classes and workshops on various mental health topics and is a board member for several community/volunteer organizations. Ann is a mother of an adult son.

CHRISTIE GAUSE-BEMIS, MSW, LCSW

Christie takes a passionate stand for women to live a life they desire. She is the co-creator of Hot Pink YOUniversity where women can find a powerful tribe to find passion, purpose and play. She is a writer, artist, traveler and mama. Through her years in private practice as a psychotherapist she has developed tools and inspired ways to facilitate transformation for women. She has her bachelor's degree from UW-Madison and her Master's degree from UW-Milwaukee. She helps women raise the quality of their lives through engaging workshops, seminars, speaking and personal coaching. Inviting women to light up their lives. Travel is a big passion and she has seen and volunteered on trips to places such as: Vietnam, Bali, Italy and Greece, Turkey, India, and many more.

ACKNOWLEDGEMENTS

As you move through life, there are people there who have your back and help you along the way. We would like to each spend some time acknowledging the sparks in our lives. To Chris and Debbie O'Byrne at Jetlaunch Publishing, our vision is in your hands. To Kathy Sparrow for the initial edits, encouragements and help in getting into the publishing world. To Lori and Diane for a shared enthusiasm and vision in the very beginning and the wisdom and courage to recognize along the way, the importance of following your own paths and passions. To Ann's Aunt Elizabeth Lopez-Murgatroyd for your wisdom, passion and Costa Rican hospitality in the very beginning. It was an incredible, inspirational experience.

From Christie: Thanks to Jana Stanfield for opening me up to travel in new and valuable transformative ways…and for opening me up to all of my fellow travelers on those wonderful trips. Thanks to Sage Lavine for her leadership and supportive programs, truly the launch and teachings I needed. And, again, for opening me up to the amazing women who are attracted to your teachings. I thank my mom for her constant support and deep wisdom. My husband and my kids, Emma, Johanna, Seth, Luke and Maya for the laughter and the joy. It is always fun to have partners in the live out loud life. And to my greatest co-creator, playmate in pleasure-seeking and co-conspirator in adventure, a big juicy thank you to Ann, what a joy-filled ride.

From Ann: Thanks and deepest gratitude to Pamela Madsen for opening me even wider to the power I hold in my own sensuality and to being a pioneer in the work that is my passion. To the brilliant, bold women of my family that came before

Acknowledgements

me- Lela Potter-Winn for saying yes to your own desires and publishing your personal story in your late 80's, instilling my desire to write and Auril Winn-Murgatroyd for leading by example as a female entrepreneur beginning in the 1950's and throughout your career. To my father, Dave Murgatroyd for being the first truly Hot Pink Dude in my life. To my mother Gloria Malcolm-Murgatroyd for showing me such strength and bravery in the face of tragedy. To my son Grant David Soe for being the love of my heart and becoming an incredibly strong and compassionate difference maker in this world. To my lover Joel for being my heart home, for how we live outloud and on fire together and for how you share your love in this world. To my amazing siblings and our loving little family for being my cornerstone and loving me as I am and in all that I do. To my bold, beautiful, brilliant soul sister-partner on this live outloud journey-you make my heart sing, my creativity expand and my vulnerable self feel honored and safe. Thanks Christie for busting our dreams wide open with me. To all those whose paths have crossed mine along the way and sparked me on this incredible journey-my heart is full.

www.ingramcontent.com/pod-product-compliance
Lightning Source LLC
Chambersburg PA
CBHW041621220426
43662CB00001B/5